Leadership Skills for Boosting Performance

Terry Gillen is a consultant trainer and author specialising in programmes that improve people's performance, effectiveness and well-being at work. He is a Fellow of, and Registered Consultant with, the Chartered Institute of Personnel and Development and a Member of the Institute of Management. His career in training began more than 20 years ago and has covered the public sector, the private sector and consultancy. As well as running courses throughout the United Kingdom, he has taught in Europe and the Far East. Terry is a prolific writer whose works have been translated into a total of 16 languages. His previous books for the CIPD include *Agreed! Improve your powers of influence* (1999) and, in the popular 'Management Shapers' series, *The Appraisal Discussion* (1998) and *Assertiveness* (1998). He has been a subject expert adviser on e-learning programmes and has produced a number of training resources for the CIPD, including *Exercises for Interpersonal Skills Training* (2000), *Exercises in Appraisal and Performance Development* (1999) and, with John Adair, *Adair's Management and Development Exercises* (1997). He can be contacted at PO Box 585, Tring, Hertfordshire, HP23 5SX.

As always, to my family

The Chartered Institute of Personnel and Development is the leading publisher of books and reports for personnel and training professionals, students, and all those concerned with the effective management and development of people at work. For details of all our titles, please contact the Publishing Department:

tel. 020-8263 3387

fax 020-8263 3850

e-mail publish@cipd.co.uk

The catalogue of all CIPD titles can be viewed on the CIPD website:

www.cipd.co.uk/publications

Leadership Skills for Boosting Performance

Terry Gillen

CHARTERED INSTITUTE OF PERSONNEL AND DEVELOPMENT

Typesetting by Wyvern 21 Ltd, Bristol
and printed in Great Britain by
the Cromwell Press, Trowbridge, Wiltshire

British Library Cataloguing in Publication Data
A catalogue record for this book is available from the British Library

ISBN 0-85292-924-2

Chartered Institute of Personnel and Development, CIPD House,
Camp Road, London SW19 4UX
Tel: 020-8971 9000   Fax: 020-8263 3333
E-mail: cipd@cipd.co.uk
Website: www.cipd.co.uk
Incorporated by Royal Charter. Registered charity no. 1079797.

Contents

Preface

Another book on leadership?
Yes, but this one is different...

Too much writing on leadership focuses on tearing up the rule book and turning your organisation on its head. Or it describes the impressive antics of maverick chief executive officers (CEOs) or the daring exploits of astounding explorers. These books can provide insight and inspiration but can be of questionable value in terms of practical guidance.

Practical leadership boils down to two things: efficiently managing performance-related processes and connecting people's emotions to the results you need them to achieve. It sounds simple when you say it like that. It just happens to be incredibly elusive. Making it accessible to you in such a way that you can put it into practice quickly and easily is what this book is all about.

My publishers tell me they expect a wide range of people to read this book. If I can make so bold as to put you into one of three categories, I shall welcome you personally. The categories are:

  - chief executives and senior managers
  - human resource (HR) specialists
  - line managers.

If you are a chief executive or senior manager

I meet a lot of CEOs and senior managers who, quite rightly, want a business case to support people initiatives. So here are the reasons I believe we dare not delay in taking a serious look at the leadership quality of our managers.

As a CEO or senior manager, you are probably used to thinking strategically about your organisation. You might be used to considering issues such as outsourcing, value chain partners, reorganisations, new investments, mergers and acquisitions, global competition and so on. Yet some of the most significant changes affecting organisations today are happening right under our noses. They affect our people and the fundamental nature of the employer/employee relationship.

Technology is changing the way our organisations function. There is more downsizing, more delayering, more empowerment, more mobility, more home working, more globalisation, more teamworking and so on. But there is also less traditional work activity and less control of remote staff, mobile staff and the staff of strategic partners. There is less of an umbilical-like attachment between employer and employee – and this has serious implications for staff loyalty and retention, especially in view of increasing skills shortages.

> '*People do not want to put life on hold Monday to Friday; they want work to add to their life experience.*'

The tail end of the 20th century saw a build-up of work pressures on individuals and a growing debate about the need for a balance between work and life outside work. High salaries have proved insufficient to retain good staff. Talented people demand more than fair remuneration: they demand the kind of 'climate' in which they can enjoy their work, develop their skills, establish satisfying relationships and feel that what they do is meaningful and that they are respected for their contribution. In short, people do not want to put life on hold Monday to Friday; they want work to add to their life experience. We are entering a new paradigm in which talented people 'hire' their employer, not vice versa.

According to research from Harvard University, much of an organisation's climate can be traced to the leadership style of its managers. And this is true in all sectors. Yet far too often we still reward managers for control of easily measurable day-to-day detail, so encouraging them to focus on that area. But we rarely measure, or encourage managers to focus on, ideas, values, feelings and morale.

At a corporate level we still tend to value companies in terms of what they own, produce and sell. We ignore the fact that customers and employees assess them in a totally different way. Their assessments are based on what the organisation is like to interact with. Hence the growing interest in intellectual capital (IC) – the worth of the organisation's intangible assets.

Much of an organisation's intellectual capital lies between the ears of its employees. It is what they know, how they work together and how they interact with customers. Intellectual capital is regarded as sufficiently important in some countries (such as Sweden, Norway and Japan) for companies' IC ratings to be published alongside their financial ratings, because there is a good correlation between a company's IC rating and the steadiness of its stock value. Yet still we tend to focus more attention on external issues than on this crucial internal challenge – developing the kind of manager/staff relationship applicable to the way organisations increasingly function and the work/life expectations of staff.

Enhancing managers' leadership skills is central to the twin goals of strengthening the employer/employee bond among talented staff and of boosting everyone's performance. It deserves a place high up the corporate agenda.

If you are in HR

I meet a lot of specialists in HR who sincerely want to make a difference to their organisations' performance. They invest time, money and effort in appraisal systems, teambuilding activities, leadership programmes, rebranding values and more. Yet, often, these initiatives miss something fundamental – what really boosts performance is the relationship between managers and their staff.

> *⁶There is nothing wrong with well-meaning initiatives, but unless they affect the relationship between staff and managers, the staff will never achieve their full potential.⁹*

That relationship is about connecting people to performance in the most effective way possible. Yet too often the revamped appraisal system still looks like a once-a-year event owned by HR; everyone enjoys the leadership programme but the attendees' staff see no difference; and the vision and values statement fails to percolate its way into measures against which people are actually assessed. There is nothing wrong with well-meaning initiatives, but unless they affect the relationship between managers and staff they will never achieve their full potential.

This book focuses on the manager–staff relationship and provides practical and tested guidance. As you read it you can benefit in two ways. First, as a manager and leader yourself, you can work on your relationship with your own staff. Second, as an HR specialist, you can influence the relationship other managers have with their staff.

If you are a manager
You could be reading this book for several reasons.

- You are in your first management role and want to succeed.
- You have been managing for years but it seems to be getting more difficult.
- You are under pressure and need to achieve tougher targets.
- You are leading a new team and want to get off to a good start.
- You want to be a better manager.
- You would like your staff to feel that you are the best boss they have ever had.

Whatever your reasons, you are probably looking for something that is easy but not superficial, that is simple but incisive and that is intriguing but practical. That is what I have set out to write.

> *When people tell you they have learned more in the past hour than they learned at a prestigious management college, you begin to feel that you are onto something.*

When people on courses tell you that what they have learned in the past hour has been of more practical value than what they learned during five days at a prestigious management college, or that they wonder where they might have been now if only they had known this stuff when they were starting their careers, you begin to feel that you are onto something.

Yet that 'something' is not based on a PhD thesis that has been given a marketing make-over to become the latest management fad. Neither is it based on interviews with leaders of global companies or others whose activities have little in common with yours. It is based on observation and feedback from many managers and staff over many years on what genuinely makes a difference.

You could say that making a difference is the bottom line of management. If, by your presence and actions, you make a difference to people's performance, job satisfaction, careers and sense of well-being at work, then you are a good manager. In the same way that you can probably still remember the schoolteacher who made a positive difference for you many years ago, wouldn't it be nice if your staff were to remember the positive difference you make for them many years into the future?

If you picked up this book because you wanted something that will make a difference for you, I guess you could say that your future is in your hands right now.

'Whichever of these categories you are in, welcome to the book!'

Introduction

> *Despite major advances in technology, staff and their performance are still central to organisational success.*

Most managers know that organisations increasingly have to respond to developments such as global competition, pressure to reduce costs, the '24-hour economy', rising customer expectations and e-commerce. Yet despite major advances in processes and technology, staff and their performance are still central to organisational success. And, because managers are the link between staff and their performance, the better the manager, the better the performance. This book identifies and explains the crucial but neglected steps in raising your game to a new level: to growing from a manager into a leader.

What does it mean to be a manager?

I believe that simplicity and clarity go together. In more than 20 years of involvement in management development, I have discovered that managers become more effective when they understand some simple but, at first, not very obvious facts about their role.

So let's get straight to the heart of the problem – few of us enter our trade or profession because we want to be a manager. We go into medicine, law, architecture, engineering, information technology (IT), charity work or the Church because we want to *do things* related to that subject. Then, as a result of our success *doing things*, we get promoted. So now we have to *manage processes* as well. (I say 'as well' because even very senior managers seem to spend some of their time doing things.) *Managing processes* usually involves staff, so let's distinguish that part from managing processes by adding *leading people*. You can divide a manager's job into three parts: doing things, managing processes and leading people.

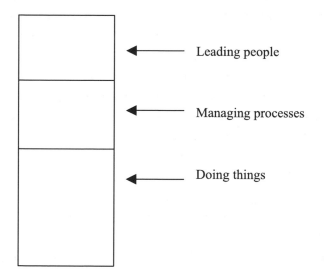

Now think about this: *doing things* is what attracted us to our trade or profession in the first place, and it is what we are so good at that we got promoted. Consequently, it is a major comfort zone for us. *Managing processes*, while necessary, is difficult to get excited about. Be honest, have you ever known anyone get excited by spreadsheets, schedules and projections? It is, however, a relatively comfortable hiding place if you are bothered by the third part of the job, *leading people*. This is a major discomfort zone for many managers because it is the breeding ground of so many performance and relationship problems. Not only is it fraught with problems, it takes managers away from doing the things they like!

Yet it is also the bit of the job with the greatest potential for performance improvement, satisfying relationships and enhanced credibility. Let's take performance improvement first.

Performance improvement

Organisations exist for a very simple reason – to turn resources into something of value. This applies whether your organisation is in the commercial sector, public sector or voluntary sector. Your organisation might be turning metal into motor cars, taxes into clean streets or donations into a good cause. Whatever it is, the organisation puts the resources through various processes to turn them into the desired output. People handle the processes and the better they handle them the better the organisation performs. The person with the greatest influence on how well people handle the processes is their manager.

Think of performance as a weight and your management activities as the lever with which you lift the weight. The weight is getting heavier all the time and, as demands for improved performance continue unabated, you only have two choices: you can work even harder (which is an unappealing prospect for most of us) or you can lift the increased weight by making the lever longer and applying the same effort. In other words, you can work smarter.

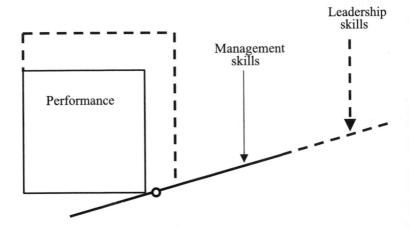

Working smarter is not as elusive as it might sound. Have you ever shopped at a supermarket, got home and, realising you have been overcharged, returned to the supermarket and given them a hard time? They have had to run around checking till receipts, questioning staff, involving supervisors and so on. It would have been easier for them (and you) to have got it right first time. The procedures, training and attitudes that would have enabled them to get it right first time come under the heading 'working smarter'.

Whenever managers train their staff, pass on helpful procedures or instil the skills, confidence and authority to make decisions, they improve performance. If the managers go on to create an environment in which staff work as a team and feel an emotional connection to performance goals, they achieve superior results without extra effort. That is working smarter or, in our analogy, using leadership leverage to achieve better performance.

Satisfying relationships

We human beings are just as efficient at learning the wrong thing as we are at learning the right thing. Imagine two managers, both new to their posts and keen to maintain tight control over their staff until they get to know them. They both insist that their staff bring problems and decisions to them. When the first manager's staff come to him, he tells them in detail what they must do. When the second manager's staff come to her, she discusses the problems and decisions with them and helps them work out what to do.

After a month the first manager is complaining that he has a poor team, he cannot trust them, he has to do their work for them and so on. With him they have learned not to think, to feel unsure about their ability and to delegate upwards in case they do something wrong. The second manager feels comfortable with her team and enjoys good relationships with them. With her they have learned to think, to be confident and to feel supported.

> ‘All interaction between you and your staff achieves something
> The question is, does it achieve what you want it to?’

As adults, we spend a significant amount of our waking hours at work. We are also gregarious beings who thrive on satisfying relationships. Managers who operate as the performance police officer establish less satisfying relationships with their staff than managers who operate as the performance coach.

Enhanced credibility

Ask yourself this simple but telling question: if your staff had a choice, would they choose you as their manager? Or would they choose someone who helped them to achieve superior performance and to feel good about doing so? Superior performance and feeling good are not mutually exclusive. The members of high-performing teams usually feel good about their achievements and about working together. They also feel pretty good about their team leader.

Your credibility has three main sources: your technical ability, your position in the hierarchy and how your staff feel about you. The first is less important than it used to be. In these days of rapid technological advances, wide spans of control and empowerment, staff often know more than their managers. The second is less important than it used to be. As a society, we just do not doff our caps to authority the way we used to. The third – the way your staff feel about you – will be a direct result of how you make them feel when you interact with them.

There is also the issue of your credibility among more senior managers. If you were a senior manager, whom would you rate: a manager whose staff were firing on all cylinders or one whose staff were digging tunnels trying to escape? You choose.

Conclusion

So what does it mean to be a manager? It means that a substantial part of your job lies in connecting the emotions of your staff to the processes and results the organisation needs to achieve. It means that if you are not careful you can gravitate towards the tempting comfort zones of doing things and managing processes rather than the high-performance leverage zone of leading people. It also means that you have an opportunity to positively influence the satisfaction you and your staff gain from a major part of your lives.

As you read on, you will discover how to transform your own thinking, acquire practical 'working smarter' skills and boost staff performance. You will also enhance your credibility amongst staff, peers and others. Finally, as practical leadership skills are so scarce, you will probably find you become more sought after and more marketable.

The rest of this book is divided into four parts:

- tactics that will help you clarify performance expectations with staff
- probably the most practical ideas for developing staff performance you have ever come across
- insights that will enable you to transform a small step into a giant leap by making easy but powerful changes to your management/ leadership style
- advice on how to capitalise on the numerous opportunities when your leadership credibility is on the line and emerge from them an even more respected leader.

1

Clarifying performance expectations

One of the most fundamental problems I see in management is a lack of clarity between managers and their staff as to what performance is expected and how it will be assessed. That lack of clarity has a detrimental effect on performance, motivation, appraisals, relationships with staff and your credibility. It makes the performance lever (see page xviii) shorter.

Clarifying performance expectations, however, goes beyond increasing the chances of getting high performance: if the performance-clarification process is handled positively, you also get motivation, credibility and relationship benefits. In other words, there is a lot at stake. What you will find interesting is that getting it wrong actually consumes more time and effort than getting it right.

Something else you will find interesting is that the presence of job descriptions and appraisal systems does not make the difference to performance clarification that you might expect. The two things that make a big difference, however, are thinking and discussing.

The thinking part

The thinking part concerns you clarifying in your own mind the performance and behaviour that make a real difference. It is quite easy to do as long as you think about performance holistically.

Thinking holistically

I can best explain holistic performance with an example. Let's say you have a choice of going to either of two dentists. Both are equally convenient, equally expensive and equally competent. What would make you choose one rather than the other? The chances are that your answer will boil down to how the winning dentist makes you feel. Are you welcomed as you go in? Is the waiting room comfortable? As you lie in the chair do you feel as if you are valued and that the dentist has your best interests at heart? Is being in the presence of that dentist a relatively pleasant experience? Even for those of us with a high pain threshold, these things are important.

Dentists who want to increase their business need to think this way but, because they went into dentistry to work with teeth, there is a danger that they might not consider these other matters unless they think holistically about their performance.

Thinking holistically about performance simply means thinking about technical skills, personal skills and inputs and outputs. While, in the final analysis, it is only the outputs that we want, sometimes it pays to focus our attention on the inputs and allow the outputs to take care of themselves. Athletes, for example, focus intently on how they hold a javelin and run up to the line or on their approach to the high-jump bar, knowing that by improving the inputs they are making improved outputs possible.

Once you are thinking holistically, you can also think descriptively.

Thinking descriptively

Thinking descriptively will help you avoid the trap of discussing performance expectations in terms that are subjective and general. Words like 'maximum', 'best', 'efficient' and 'effective' are too vague to clarify performance expectations. You need to be specific and objective. It is easier than it sounds.

Imagine three fictitious members of staff. The performance of the first one is fine – nothing special, but perfectly satisfactory. The performance of the second gives cause for concern: some aspects are what you would expect from someone new to the post rather than an experienced person, and some aspects are plainly unacceptable. The performance of the third member of staff is better than you could reasonably expect: in fact, if more of your staff could perform at this level you would be a very happy manager indeed.

As long as the descriptions of the three fictitious members of staff include technical skills, personal skills, inputs and outputs, you have just described the three performance levels crucial to clarifying performance expectations. The figure overleaf shows you a simple template for thinking about these descriptions, while the table on pages 4–6 gives you a list of some of the technical skills, personal skills, inputs and outputs you can include in your holistic descriptions.

Better than acceptable ☺	*Nnnnnnnnnnnnnnnnnnnn* *Nnnnnnnnnnnnnnnnnnnn* *Nnnnnnnnnnnnnnnnnnnn*
Acceptable ☹	*Nnnnnnnnnnnnnnnnnnnn* *Nnnnnnnnnnnnnnnnnnnn* *Nnnnnnnnnnnnnnnnnnnn*
Less than acceptable ☹	*Nnnnnnnnnnnnnnnnnnnn* *Nnnnnnnnnnnnnnnnnnnn* *nnnnnnnnnnnnnnnnnnnn*

Level	Indicator
Exceeds requirements	▪ Excellent technical ability; often sought after by others for advice ▪ Exceeds personal objectives; makes a substantial contribution to team objectives ▪ 'Runs the extra mile'; can always be relied upon to help out with problems ▪ Accepts responsibility, solves problems and makes decisions at a level one would expect from a more senior person ▪ Owns problems, even helping others to meet deadlines and fulfil customer expectations ▪ Sees the bigger picture; understands, and takes account of, implications for others ▪ Applies him/herself well; manages time very effectively

Level	Indicator
	■ An ambassador for the team and company when dealing with customers
	■ Positive attitude; causes others to think positively
Meets requirements	■ Technically competent
	■ Meets majority of personal objectives; contributes to team objectives
	■ Conscientious
	■ Tidy; appearance appropriate
	■ Hardworking; uses time satisfactorily
	■ Accepts responsibility; takes ownership of issues and problems
	■ Willing to help out in problem situations
	■ Provides good customer service
	■ Solves problems and makes decisions within capabilities
	■ Positive attitude
	■ Good team player; gets on well with other team members
	■ Impartial when dealing with staff and colleagues
	■ Reliable in routine situations
Fails requirements	■ Technical competence below requirements
	■ Error rate, rectification rate or quality poor
	■ Work rate lower than ability and/or staff in same or similar jobs
	■ Does the minimum to get by
	■ Unreliable
	■ Untidy worker; appearance below acceptable level
	■ Avoids responsibility

Level	Indicator
	■ Avoids helping out in problem situations
	■ Shows less initiative than he/she has potential for
	■ Parochial; refuses to think beyond own boundaries
	■ Customer care falls short of desired levels
	■ Has 'favourites' (staff and/or colleagues)
	■ Negative attitude (eg looks for problems, 'anti' company initiatives)
	■ Causes others to think negatively
	■ Contributes little to team efforts

Note: These indicators are general and are meant to raise your awareness of what to look for when developing and assessing people's performance. Individual circumstances, and hence expectations, vary greatly. The boundary between one level and the next will involve shades of grey rather than black and white issues. So always seek guidance from your personnel manager before taking any action affecting the nature of someone's employment.

Having thought through what performance you want from staff, the next stage is to communicate it to them.

The discussing part

Through discussion you and your staff can achieve a common understanding of performance expectations. Discussing performance with staff rather than just telling them what you want has several benefits.

■ Your thinking will probably be fine-tuned and enhanced by what they say. Discussing performance expectations almost always makes those expectations more incisive and comprehensive.

- Staff are more inclined to accept your views, because people naturally resist anything they feel is being forced on them, yet we naturally 'own' something we have helped to create.
- Discussion, listening and agreement help build relationships.

It is worthwhile, at this stage, to remember where this fits into being a better manager. The managing things part of your job requires you to achieve certain performance outcomes. The leading people part of your job is the way you do it. Clarifying performance expectations is an important part of the way you bring the two together.

To encourage and help you, your organisation might have an appraisal process: appraisal system, staff report, performance review – whatever its name, the principle is the same. The organisation is encouraging you to clarify performance expectations and give staff feedback on their performance. Whether you have a formal process or not, the 'better manager' principles are the same: as a manager you need to clarify performance expectations. One of the ways in which you can clarify performance expectations further is to agree objectives and/or performance standards with staff.

Objectives

You may already be comfortable with objective-setting, but are you aware of the two big potential problems when discussing objectives with staff? Understanding them will help you avoid them.

Agreeing pantomime objectives

These are objectives that are so subjective and general that conversations reviewing performance degenerate into the kind of dialogue you hear during a Christmas pantomime. For example: 'We agreed that you would contribute to team effectiveness.' 'I have.' 'Oh no you haven't.' 'Oh yes I have.' 'Oh no you haven't.' To overcome this problem it is easy to go to the other extreme and only agree objectives that are easily quantified. That, however, can lead to the second problem.

Incorrectly quantifying objectives

This problem is more difficult to spot because the objectives look right. So let's look at some real examples. First, we know that hospital administrators have objectives relating to reducing the number of patients on waiting lists. It might concern you to learn that some hospitals have spotted that the objective relates to the number of patients on the waiting lists and not to the severity of patients' conditions. They are, therefore, instructing clinicians to see greater numbers of patients, which they can only do by giving preference to patients with simple ailments. (Yes, the patients with more serious conditions might become so ill they are admitted through Accident and Emergency – but that is a different set of figures.)

Second, police forces have objectives relating to crimes detected per 100 officers, but would you want police officers redeployed from crime prevention, which is difficult to quantify and therefore is not measured, and put on crime detection just because it is easier to quantify? Third, airline maintenance managers have been known to refuse to send technicians to repair aeroplanes until the following day because the overnight accommodation and overtime payments would come from their budgets. The fact that another airline department has to shoulder the much greater cost of recompensing disgruntled passengers does not relate to their objectives.

> *What gets measured gets done. So if you measure the wrong things, you get the wrong things done.*

In schools, for example, an easily quantifiable performance measure is examination success. If that is all we measure, however, schools will deliver the better examination results by preventing less able students from sitting exams and by ensuring that students spend less time on music, sport, drama, the development of social skills and other aspects of a well-rounded education.

The purpose of objectives is to focus people's efforts, give them something to 'go for'. Pantomime objectives do not do that and incorrectly quantified objectives may deliver the performance you do not want. So how can you avoid these problems? Here are some thoughts. First, agree a mix of objectives from the following list:

- 'Hard' objectives usually refer to something, often *quantifiable*, that must be achieved.
- 'Soft' objectives usually refer to activities that, while important, are difficult or unproductive to quantify. They often describe how someone goes about his or her job. They work best when they are *descriptive* rather than numerical.

- Personal development objectives relate to a skill or knowledge that, if developed, will improve the inputs and, consequently, the outputs.
- Team objectives are more useful than individual objectives in some situations, such as those in which people work more as a team and in which the team's performance is more important to improved outputs than any one individual's performance.
- Finally, you can consider performance standards. Strictly speaking, they are not objectives; they are descriptions of levels of performance below which a performance or behaviour should not fall. They are appropriate where less than acceptable performance on a particular task would be significant but where better than acceptable performance is either impossible or unnecessary. Examples include answering the telephone within a certain number of rings or following a procedure.

Second, use a framework when discussing and agreeing objectives. The SMART framework is one of the best. You will see what SMART (enhanced from Paul J Meyer's original) stands for in the table opposite.

While discussing performance expectations, there are two more things to discuss and agree: how you will monitor performance and how you will help your staff achieve good performance.

SMART	Notes
Specific and stretching	If they are not specific they will end up as pantomime objectives. Being specific aids clarity and understanding. 'Stretching' recognises that people grow and develop and that reaching a stretching goal provides a sense of achievement.
Measurable and motivating	Measurable makes the objective even more specific, and hence clearer. For some topics, however, a descriptive objective can be more useful than a quantified one. For example, improving staff morale from *description* to *description* will be more useful than choosing some numerical barometer of morale.
Achievable and agreed	When we feel an objective cannot be achieved, we do not rise to the challenge. We throttle back, knowing there is no point in trying. Staff have to believe that an objective can be achieved. Hence the need for dialogue and, sometimes, compromise. People resist objectives that are imposed on them but accept those they help determine.
Relevant and reinforced	Good objectives focus people's efforts, and effort is a scarce commodity. You can't afford to waste it on anything that is not relevant to overall goals. People do not exist in a vacuum. We need feedback, help and encouragement to reinforce our efforts.
Timed and trackable	Timescales assist clarity still further and help staff organise their time. 'Trackable' means knowing whether you and your staff can track their progress towards the objective. If you can, you get the many benefits of monitoring performance.

Monitoring performance

Monitoring performance gives you opportunities to tackle problems while they are still small, spot learning and development needs that will benefit from immediate attention, use feedback to modify behaviour and capitalise on spontaneous coaching opportunities.

How you agree to monitor staff performance will depend on the nature of the work and the culture of your organisation but, again, it will help you gain maximum benefit from this book if you follow certain principles. Performance monitoring works best when it:

- happens quickly
- is accurate and believed
- is relatively easy to collect and collate
- is 'owned' by the people whose performance it is describing
- is as user-friendly as possible.

Collecting information that is then sent to an IT department, analysed and returned as a printout a month later is a surprisingly common method of monitoring performance. It is not only counter to the five principles described above, it also fails to involve staff in their own performance fine-tuning. When people feel that performance fine-tuning is something that is done to them rather than something in which they are fully involved, they tend to feel alienated from the process, resent those associated with it and resist suggestions that would otherwise help them. Consequently, they perform below their potential.

When, on the other hand, they are fully involved in the process, they tend to feel part of it, see the benefits for themselves and the company, and use their initiative more. This makes it easier for them to fulfil their performance potential – especially if you give feedback on their performance the right way.

Helping staff with performance feedback

Good-quality feedback is specific rather than vague, descriptive rather than woolly and factual rather than subjective. Vague, woolly and subjective feedback, even if it praises an individual's work, is always a demotivator because the underlying message is that the manager does not understand the staff member's performance. Which feedback would you rather receive, the one on the left or the one on the right?

■ 'That was quite good.'	■ 'That report was very thorough. The statistics added credibility to your conclusion.'
■ 'You are a valuable member of the team.'	■ 'The more junior team members often seek your advice and you help them make good decisions.'
■ 'Your performance has been satisfactory.'	■ 'You had some tough objectives and, by carefully targeting your effort and seeking advice in good time when you encountered difficulties, your performance remained well within acceptable limits.'

Feedback has more impact when it follows the few simple rules you will see in the table opposite.

> *'It is a "law" of the universe that good-quality feedback improves performance.'*

There is no doubt that good-quality feedback improves performance. By clarifying performance expectations, genuinely discussing those expectations with staff, agreeing between you how you can monitor and support their efforts and giving them good-quality feedback, you are well on the way to being an exceptional people manager. You can take it a step further, however, by deliberately developing their performance potential.

Critical feedback	Positive feedback
■ Remember that the purpose of critical feedback is to modify other people's behaviour, not to vent your emotions.	■ Remember the purpose of positive feedback is to encourage more of the same behaviour by reinforcing it.
■ Describe the behaviour/results you are observing.	■ Describe the behaviour/results you are praising.
■ Check that your observations are correct.	■ Explain how you feel about the behaviour/results.
■ Listen to any mitigating circumstances.	■ If relevant, explore what staff did to achieve the behaviour/results and discuss in what other situations they might do the same.
■ Describe accurately and concisely what you want.	
■ Check that staff will do what you want	
■ Thank them in advance.	■ Thank them and encourage more of the same.
■ Stay focused on behaviour/results; don't drift into personal comments.	

2

Developing performance potential

Some managers do not see staff development as part of their job. They see it as HR's job or, now that the era of 'Me plc' has affected traditional career paths, they see it as each individual's responsibility. Some managers even believe that by developing their staff they will simply lose them sooner and never recoup the investment. These issues distract us from the key point that better performance through working smarter rather than harder benefits everyone. So let's examine them.

Whose responsibility?

When managers see only the doing things and managing processes parts of their job, they fail to realise that they are the prime beneficiary of staff development. I say this because if you develop workers' personal skills as well as their technical skills:

- they are more able to perform above acceptable levels (see table, pages 4–6).
- they are more able to work smarter, making the lever longer (see figure, page xviii)
- you have more time available to develop your own skills.

So, whether you accept the responsibility or not, you certainly have a lot to gain.

Is it worth the investment if they leave you?

There are three more benefits. First, according to research conducted independently by Coopers & Lybrand in the USA and by the Institute of Employment Studies in the UK, developing staff increases staff retention rather than reduces it. For as long as developing staff stay, you will probably get more energy and enthusiasm from them than their remuneration may warrant. Second, when they do move on they may act as ambassadors for your organisation. Third, because of your reputation as a people developer, you can select the best replacement from the long queue of eager applicants. The alternative is to employ staff whose energy and enthusiasm are less than you might expect for what you are paying them and who finally leave in desperation. You then have to select a replacement from the 'walking wounded', because good applicants prefer to work for good managers.

So is it worth it? Look at the table opposite. It is a list of the indicators that development has taken place. Ask yourself how you, your team's performance and your reputation would benefit if your staff could demonstrate just a few of these indicators.

Workplace development

So, having established that staff development is a good thing, what is the best way of doing it? Generally, we rely too much on courses. Courses can be useful and they are usually fun, but in terms of achieving any of the 11

1 Increased quantity or quality of output
2 Increased mastery of task; improved consistency of good results
3 More initiative, better decisions
4 Larger perspective will be evident; staff will think beyond previous boundaries; staff will be able to manage situations that would previously have caused confusion, problems, requests for help or managerial intervention; staff will think both long- and short-term
5 More noticeable creativity in response to problems and new situations
6 More and better use of people networks, inside and outside the organisation, resulting in greater achievement
7 Sense of personal growth; staff can cite examples of what they are achieving now that, say, 12 months before would have been beyond their ability
8 Staff can be given or considered for tasks which, say, 12 months ago would have been beyond their ability
9 Staff can successfully take on higher-profile, riskier or more important tasks
10 Staff can cite examples of what has been learned, how it has been employed and the results that have been achieved
11 Staff are increasingly sought out by others for help, advice and guidance

development indicators in the table above, their success rate can leave a lot to be desired. So, while courses have their place, they also have their limitations. Seeing courses as the only development method is like channelling all traffic along a narrow, single-track road while an adjacent motorway is virtually empty. The big development opportunities occur in the workplace.

We have begun to realise in recent years that the workplace is a rich source of free and convenient development opportunities if only we recognise them as such. To do so, we have to distinguish between accidental learning and deliberate learning.

Accidental learning is what we usually mean when we talk about learning from experience. The limitation, however, is that we are just as adept at learning the wrong things as we are at learning the right things. If, for example, an experience is unpleasant, we can just as easily learn to avoid it in future as we can learn how to handle it better in future. This makes accidental learning a bit hit and miss. When learning is deliberate, however, we can not only squeeze maximum learning value from experiences, we can select learning experiences in advance.

The table below shows a range of typical workplace activities and the potential learning they can contain. The essential points to grasp are that:

- working and learning need not be two separate activities
- by thinking of deliberate learning rather than accidental learning, you can get the job done and develop your staff simultaneously.

Please remember, however, that you will need to tailor your approach to the situation. Specifically, consider the staff member's competence in relation to the task, the risk inherent in the task (that is, the combination of the likelihood of problems and the consequences of those problems) and, finally, the confidence of both you and the staff member in a satisfactory outcome.

Workplace activity	Potential learning
Being involved in or leading a project; participating in or leading a multi-functional task force	Greater knowledge of the subject; planning skills; interpersonal skills; appreciation of other functions
Special studies or investigations	In-depth subject knowledge; planning skills; report writing; presentation skills
Chairing a meeting	People skills, problem-solving and decision-making
Providing holiday cover	Knowledge of the job or tasks for which they are providing cover
Being delegated to	Knowledge, skills and attitudes associated with the delegated task
Being forced to delegate	How to coach staff; benefits of operating at a higher level/with greater leverage

Workplace activity	Potential learning
Coaching or mentoring other staff	Teaching skills; people skills
Assisting or working with external consultants	New ways of working, wider perspective
Preparing a budget, marketing plan, geographical study, competitor analysis, policy statement or recommendations to senior management	Knowledge of budgeting, marketing and so on; appreciation of wider issues
Analysing markets, competitors, trends, best practice and so on	Better knowledge of industry, external issues and so on
Benchmarking against another person, section, department, organisation and so on	Improved knowledge of good practice, fresh perspective
Participating in contract negotiations	Legal knowledge; budget knowledge; influencing skills
Troubleshooting problems	Investigative skills; technical knowledge; problem-solving and decision-making skills; people skills
Staffing a stand at a trade show	Product knowledge; customer knowledge; interpersonal skills

Workplace activity	Potential learning
Teaching or coaching other people; developing a training programme	Better understanding of subject matter; people skills Taking on a bigger job
Giving a speech or presentation	Presentation skills; organising skills; self-confidence; audience requirements
Working with people from different functions and cultures or who have different views	Broader view of organisational requirements; influencing skills
Installing a new system	Improved technical knowledge; planning skills; organising skills; influencing skills
Acting as 'assistant to' for a specified period orpurpose	Experience of wider issues; knowledge of different working practices
Recruiting new staff	Understanding of longer-term organisational needs; knowledge of recruitment market and practices
Negotiating with staff groups, unions	Negotiating skills; appreciation of wider issues

Workplace activity	Potential learning
Taking on a bigger job Presentation skills; organising skills; self-confidence; audience requirements	Depends on the job but bigger jobs usually involve decisions with larger repercussions, thinking across different boundaries, more demanding people skills, organising a wide range of resources and so on
Moving to a job which is 'upstream' or 'downstream' of the current job	Better appreciation of the needs of internal customers/suppliers
Moving from a 'line' to a 'head office' job	Wider perspective of organisational needs
Moving from a 'head office' to a 'line' job	Better appreciation of life at the 'sharp end', of effects of head office decisions; people skills

At this stage, it will help you further if you understand a key point about how we learn. The figure below shows a typical learning cycle. It has four stages:

1 We decide what we are going to do.
2 We do it.
3 We receive feedback.
4 We reflect on that feedback and decide how we will improve the way we do it next time.

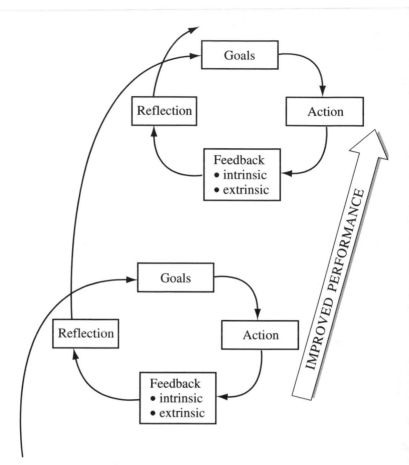

The learning cycle is not perfect, however: it has two weak links. The first is the feedback stage. If we rely on intrinsic feedback (that is, feedback from the task itself) it can be very limited. Playing snooker or pool is a good example. Seeing that a ball has missed a pocket (intrinsic feedback) does not necessarily help you work out what to do differently next time. If, however, you are being observed by other people, they might be able to give you (extrinsic) feedback on what you are doing wrong with your arm. In other words, intrinsic feedback on its own has limited value; it benefits from extrinsic feedback.

Second, far too often we like to get on with things rather than reflect on them. If we fail to reflect on the feedback and consider how to benefit from it, we do not make the leap to the next loop on the spiral. That leap to the next loop on the spiral is what we think of when we refer to development or working smarter. As a manager, there is a simple and effective way you can help your staff gain the full potential benefit from workplace development – coaching.

Coaching

Coaching is a powerful yet underused skill. It helps you turn ordinary conversations with staff into learning opportunities. It also has beneficial effects on their motivation, your relationship with them and your leadership credibility.

Coaching has its roots in sport. In sport, coaches know that, in the final analysis, it is not they who must perform, it is the people they are coaching. In work, we know that, in the final analysis, it is not managers or leaders who must perform, it is the individuals who make up the organisation. That is why more and more managers and leaders are learning from their sporting counterparts. They are learning how to coach. Here is an example.

The following dialogues represent two versions of the same conversation in which a bank clerk is seeking his manager's advice on a customer issue. Read both versions and ask yourself which one would be of greater benefit to the clerk's motivation, his development and his attitude towards his manager.

Dialogue 1

Boss, can I see you a minute, please?

Yes, how can I help?

Well, it's about these new targets we've got – the ones about referring customers with large savings in a deposit account to the unit trust adviser.

What about them?

Well…I just don't think I'll be able to achieve them.

Nonsense. A bright lad like you! You'll be able to refer lots of customers.

It's just that I feel so nervous.

Everyone has nerves. Don't worry. They'll pass, they always do.

Well, some of the customers start asking me really difficult questions – and I just don't know what to say.

You're not supposed to say anything. That's the unit trust adviser's job. They're the ones who are technically qualified, you know. If you tried to give customers advice when you're not qualified to do that, the bank could wind up in real hot water.

That's what I tell them and I can see in their eyes that they don't want to be referred. It makes me feel…well…

Come on, now. You've got to pull yourself together. This branch has got some tough targets this quarter. I'm relying on you. You're one of my best workers, you know. I've got faith in you. Now go out there, think positively and give it your best shot.

Dialogue 2

Boss, can I see you a minute, please?

Yes, how can I help?

Well, it's about these new targets we've got – the ones about referring customers with large savings in a deposit account to the unit trust adviser.

The revised targets I explained this morning. You sound concerned.

Well...I just don't think I'll be able to achieve them.

I know they're tough but you sound quite worried about them.

It's just that I feel so nervous.

What is it about the targets that makes you feel nervous?

Well, some of the customers start asking me really difficult questions and I just don't know what to say.

What kind of questions?

Oh, about rates of return, what sort of shares and in what sort of markets the money is invested, how easily they can withdraw it. Things like that.

And how do you answer such questions?

I tell them I'm not qualified to answer those questions and they'll have to see the unit trust adviser.

That's correct. All discussions like that have to be with a qualified person. Do you know why?

Because if we gave them incorrect advice and it came out that the advice came from an unqualified person the bank could be in trouble.

That's right. So what is it about the situation that makes you uncomfortable?

I don't know.

Think it through. Imagine I'm a customer now and we've just had the conversation you've described. Tell me how you feel.

Well…sort of stupid.

Why might that be?

Well, I think it's because I've started this conversation about unit trusts, you've asked me a question and now I tell you that I'm not qualified so they must be thinking why did he start the conversation in the first place?

All right. So if you give them information, whether it's correct or not, you're breaking the bank's rules, and if you don't give them information you feel a bit daft.

Yes, that's it.

What do you think the effect might be if you thought of a response other than 'I'm not qualified to give you that information'?

Like what?

I don't know. Let's think of some now. What would you like to say?

I suppose something like, 'The unit trust adviser is better qualified than I am to give you that information.' Or 'The unit trust adviser knows more about this than I do.'

That's good. How about something that makes it sound even more helpful?

I know, how about, 'To ensure that you get precise and up-to-date information I'd like our unit trust adviser to help answer your questions'?

Good. That sounds helpful but not evasive. How do you feel saying that?

All right. In fact, pretty good. I think it's quite a neat response, actually.

Would you like to try it today and let me know tonight how it feels?

Yes. I'll let you know after I've reconciled the till. Thanks, boss.

No, thank you. You thought it all through yourself. All I did was ask you a few questions. Well done.

While this second conversation takes slightly longer, it is a much more effective investment of time. The first conversation is just a waste of time. Yet it is very common. We work under such pressure these days that we often feel we have insufficient time to coach or we feel that it is our role as manager to tell staff what to do when they approach us with a problem. That is why coaching requires both the right attitudes and the right skills:

- Remember, it is easy to give someone the answer they need. Sometimes that is the correct response and sometimes it is not. But it is the easy response, which is why we rely on it too much. Consequently, we miss learning opportunities from which our staff, we and our employer could benefit.
- Remember too, that telling is not coaching. Coaching produces better-quality learning than instructing because it makes the learner think more. This increases their ownership of what they are learning, their feeling of responsibility to implement it properly and their ability to 'think on their feet' in other situations. Also, it is more motivating to be coached than to be told.

■ To coach you need to be patient and to listen actively because you have to use questions to prompt the learner's thoughts and to guide them (rather than lead them by the nose) towards a solution. The key behaviours in coaching, therefore, are probing and listening.

As you use the naturally occurring learning opportunities in and around a staff member's job and coach them to capitalise on those opportunities, you help your staff develop their skills, broaden their perspective and build ever more effective relationships. In this way you not only 'leverage' better performance from them, you will gradually create a team for whom continuous performance improvement and continuous learning are inextricably linked.

Targeting development

In addition to capitalising on workplace development and making coaching part of your management style, you will also find it useful to target development activity at the precise needs of each member of staff. While your organisation's appraisal process and your own knowledge of individuals' development needs will help you, here are some additional thoughts aimed at helping staff develop in and progress beyond certain 'levels' within an organisation. As you read them, you might be able to apply some of them to yourself.

Let's say you have members of staff in a junior or a 'trainee' role and you want them to develop in that role and to progress beyond it. How many of the following ideas are you consciously implementing?

- Help them develop their own ideas and judgement.
- Help them set, and work to, their own standards of performance – especially those related to detail and quality. To do so, they will have to think beyond the piece of work they are completing to the use that will be made of the work.
- Help them to develop their time-management skills, particularly relating to prioritising and deadlines.
- Encourage them to pre-empt problems, to use their initiative and to present you with potential solutions rather than simply bringing you problems. To do this, they will have to increase their awareness of what is going on around them. They will become better team players. Their judgement and problem-solving will improve.
- Set up a system or a routine that makes it easy for them to keep you informed. Encourage them to be proactive in communicating with you. This will encourage them to be open about problems, to seek help and advice in good time and to regard themselves as a fully paid-up member of the team.
- Let the reins get longer. Help them act on their own and to know when to seek guidance. As a general rule, estimate how long it would take them to make a mistake and halve it. That is how frequently you need to review them. When you delegate work to them, ask how frequently

they would like you to check on progress. Agree review schedules with them that gradually increase the time between reviews. Consider their increasing competence, their growing confidence, the risk associated with their work and your peace of mind. Every now and then look at their overall performance and review how the reins are getting longer and what they have learned as their competence has grown.

If you have staff in a specialist role, how many of the following ideas are you consciously implementing?

- Help them stay at the cutting edge of the discipline. This might mean allowing working time in which they can review trade or technical journals, allowing them to attend conferences or courses, encouraging them to network proactively with similar specialists from other organisations and with specialists from 'adjacent' specialisms.
- Help them focus on the most critical problems or needs of the organisation, not just the ones that turn them on. One of the characteristics that makes specialists good at their job is an enthusiasm for their specialism. This sometimes leads them to define situations in their own terms, to assume that everyone else is on their wavelength and to be intolerant of views contradictory to their own. Concentrating on the organisation's needs improves their position in

the wider team and the respect non-specialists have for them.

- Similarly, gradually expose them to other functions within the organisation so that they appreciate what their specialism means to others and integrate their specialist knowledge and skills within organisational needs.
- Help them acquire interpersonal and influencing skills. Specialists not only employ their own private jargon, indecipherable to non-specialists, they can appear very intolerant of people whose views differ from their own and can have difficulty explaining their (often valid) points to others. Interpersonal and influencing skills help them interact with others more productively.
- For similar reasons, encourage them to network within the organisation. This way, learning curves are gradual and issues discussed are rarely crucial to performance. That way, when they do encounter a crucial issue, their skills, awareness and relationships are already in place.
- Ask them to coach other people. Coaching is a very effective way of simultaneously improving interpersonal skills, of spreading specialist knowledge and of building relationships. If you do encourage such coaching, let your specialists know that it will contribute to their appraisal. Otherwise they will see it as an added burden, peripheral to their real job. They will then resent it and it will backfire.

- Help them to acquire leadership experience and to step back from some of their technical work. Specialists are understandably 'hands on' and their quality standards are often extremely high. Putting them into a leadership role (such as leading a project team) forces them to step back and guide others rather than try to do it all themselves. With the appropriate coaching, this can be a very effective way of developing people management skills.

What about poor performers?

When writing about staff development, it is easy to ignore an important category of staff – poor performers. Hopefully, they are few and far between but their impact is important. If their performance is left unaddressed it can become the norm, spread to other staff, develop into a more significant problem and so on. So who are poor performers? They are workers:

- who require constant supervision
- whose work frequently requires rectification or completion
- to whom you avoid giving tasks that they should be able to do because you cannot trust them to deliver
- who avoid unpleasant tasks
- whose work-rate creates bottlenecks
- whose judgement, initiative or willingness is below what you would reasonably expect
- who refuse to co-operate
- whose attendance, sickness or punctuality

records are unacceptable

- who avoid their fair share of the workload
- whose behaviour causes conflicts with or between other staff, customers or suppliers.

There may, of course, be justifiable reasons for some of these performance problems. An obvious example is when workers are new to a role and still learning. It is vital, therefore, that you are fair, reasonable and consistent. That means, first, ensuring that your attitude is right: focusing on getting their performance back on track is a good start. Second, it means ensuring that any action you take is right. The table beginning on page 36 will help you. It shows you the main reasons staff performance drifts off track, how you can check which reason you are dealing with and what you can do about it. It is worth emphasising that most of the reasons contained within the table are not the employees' 'fault'. Third, it means following your organisation's procedures precisely and probably involving HR at an early stage.

If they are approached constructively, the majority of poor performers can be helped back on track. Those who refuse to co-operate are a very small minority. Using the development tools recommended in this chapter to help poor performers back on track will confirm your leadership credibility. (You will find more ideas on development in Chapter 4, Moments of Truth.)

Reason for underperformance	What to look for	What to do
1 They **do not know** what you want them to achieve.	■ Past performance acceptable ■ Performance on other tasks acceptable ■ Current deterioration of performance coincides with new task ■ Frequency with which staff member checks with manager is relatively high ■ No record of role clarity having been established	This is a *communication* problem. Clarify performance descriptively and agree objectives.
2 They know what you want them to achieve but **lack the competence** to achieve it	Lack of **ability** ■ Performance on other tasks acceptable ■ Task is new to employee ■ No record of training or coaching on this task	This is a *learning* problem. Train and/or coach them.
	Lack of **aptitude** ■ Performance on other tasks acceptable ■ Task is new to staff member ■ Performance below required standard *despite* training or coaching	This is a *person/task fit* problem. Consider re-deploying the person or reallocating the task but speak to your manager and personnel first.

Reason for underperformance	What to look for	What to do
3 They know what you want them to achieve and have the competence to achieve it but **lack control** over significant factors affecting their performance	▪ Performance on other tasks acceptable ▪ Staff member usually responds to new tasks ▪ Staff member dependent on other people for all or part of task ▪ Task or procedures changed recently	This is an *interference* problem Find out what the problem is and tackle it.
4 They know what you want them to achieve, have the competence and control to achieve it, but **do not want** to achieve it. This could be because: a) they **do not understand** why it is it is important	▪ Performance on other tasks acceptable ▪ No record of role clarity having been established ▪ Behavioural evidence of lack of understanding	This is a *communication* problem (see suggested action above)

Reason for underperformance	What to look for	What to do
b) they hold **views, values or beliefs contrary to those necessary** for effective performance	▪ Behavioural evidence of contrary views, values or beliefs	This is an *attitude* problem. Check to see if they can perform acceptably under close supervision. If they can, but subsequently revert to the lower standard, you have confirmation of the cause – poor attitude. They don't want to perform! Counsel them, point out the consequences of underperformance and let them try again.
c) They are **suffering outside work problems** which they cannot help but 'bring to work' with them	▪ Past performance acceptable ▪ Performance deterioration occurred relatively quickly	This may be a *personal* problem. Seek skilled assistance from personnel.

Review

In this and the previous chapter I have given you many suggestions that will help you to clarify performance expectations and develop the performance potential of your staff. These are key skills for everyone with responsibility for staff, whether those staff report directly to you or are simply part of a temporary project team for which you are responsible. Used wisely, they will improve staff performance. To boost rather than just improve staff performance, however, you need to spice up these key skills with leadership skills. That is what we will move on to next.

3

Manager or leader?

Before we begin this chapter I want to remind you of some of the points made so far. First, your job has three parts – doing things, managing processes and leading people. Second, demands for constantly increasing performance mean you need as much performance leverage as possible. Third, developing staff performance is an important contribution to performance leverage. On its own, however, it will achieve only so much. To really boost people's performance you need to really motivate them. You need to connect them to high-performance expectations emotionally. You cannot do that by becoming a more efficient manager of processes. You can only do it by enhancing your leadership skills.

Let's begin by checking exactly what we mean by leadership.

Understanding leadership

Leadership is probably one of the most studied yet least understood topics in management. I will not pretend that I understand where others have failed, but by avoiding some attractive red herrings, I do hope to shed some light on this crucial and intriguing subject.

What do I mean by red herrings? Let's take the academic approach first. In 1981 Stogdill's *Handbook of Leadership* listed 5,000 leadership studies, and the pace has accelerated since then. We are increasingly studying more about less. I have come across research into experiences of higher states of consciousness in world-class leaders, leadership and the fundamental option of self-transcendence, and even Oedipal struggles in voluntary organisations. Would you like to give those pieces of research marks out of ten for practicality?

Alternatively, you can read the numerous autobiographies of high-flying business people or study what captains of industry do. One recent study from a UK business school examined 7,500 CEOs, chairmen and directors. With the best will in the world, however, these people have authority and freedom so far in excess of most managers that their advice is of limited practical value. Chris Argyris, the American management guru, surveyed 70 books on leadership and 'found not a single actionable idea in any of them'. Scary stuff!

So what can we do? How about building on your own experience? Check your memory banks and think of a 'best ever' leader from your own personal experience. You might have to go back a long way, though. Frequently, when I ask managers on courses to do this they have to go back to school days. (Very rarely do they mention their current manager!) The chances are that you will think of someone who:

- had a very clear goal or was totally focused on something important
- had, owing to their persistent enthusiasm and the way they interacted with you, the knack of getting you excited about that goal
- set very high standards for you (and themselves) and made you feel good about striving towards those standards
- won your respect as a person partly because they made time for you, listened to you and respected you, and partly because they were consistent in their actions
- made you feel good about the goal you were working towards, the way you were working and, above all, about yourself.

I hope you have noticed that none of this mentions typical managing processes stuff like deciding budgets, preparing spreadsheets or arranging work rotas. It is much more exciting than that.

Leadership *versus* management

How do leadership and management differ? Consider the respective origins of the two words. 'Management' comes from the Latin *manus* ('hand') and is typified by the word control. 'Leader' is related to Old Norse *leith* ('the route a ship is taking'). Think about it. Not only is one bit of sea indistinguishable from another but, at sea level, the horizon is only 13 miles (20 kilometres) away. The crew has to have a lot of faith in the captain's promises of wealth and glory and that this 'leith' will get them there.

We tend to associate management with tasks, targets, budgets, policies, procedures and keeping things steady. On the other hand, we tend to associate leadership with vision, inspiration, potential and change.

> *Managers maintain things and leaders change things.*

Furthermore, our thoughts on leadership itself are developing. At one time our leadership icons were military figures leading their troops into battle or explorers leading their cold, hungry team to success despite immense physical challenges. (For the record, I am not belittling such achievements. I gain a lot of personal inspiration from them, as my bookshelves will testify. But I am questioning the relevance of the comparison to the jobs of most managers.) Leadership icons today are much more likely to be orchestra conductors.

Orchestra conductors have to be able to 'hear' in their mind how they want the music to sound and then have to convince intelligent professionals to agree with, and even be inspired by, that 'vision' and put their heart, soul and professional pride into making it sound that way. Professional musicians tell me that this is often on a very tight budget and with severely limited rehearsal time. It does not work to pull rank and tell the musicians to play the damned notes on the music in front of them. The musicians will not die if they fail to obey. They have to *want* to do it.

When you consider how much of today's competitive strategy depends on initiatives such as customer care, quality, empowerment and self-managing teamwork you can see the similarities. None of this happens because senior managers decree it will happen; it happens because people, who at one time were thought of as order fodder, allow it to happen. It will happen successfully only if they *want* it to. This is important because of the way economies are changing.

Economic changes

At one time most wealth was generated in industries typified by economies of scale and a de-skilled, production-line workforce. Being an efficient process manager was sufficient to achieve results. But now the world is a very different place. Employees' ability to think is now a more important source of wealth generation than the machinery they operate. By way of example, Microsoft's balance sheet can only explain 3 per cent of its market worth. Things are changing even in traditional production line environments. When Toyota built their UK car plant south of Derby they had a willing supply of redundant car workers in Coventry and Birmingham. But they did not recruit them. Instead they recruited former police officers, social workers, schoolteachers and so on. They worked on the basis that teaching people to assemble motor cars is easy. Teaching people to solve problems, use initiative and work in teams is not so easy. Job analysis at Nissan's UK plant has shown that production line workers are performing tasks that at one time in a traditional car plant would have been the sole preserve of management.

> *Most managers find that the really critical aspects of staff performance cannot be obtained by compulsion.*

This alters the priority of managers' actions from organising and controlling staff to maximising their motivation and willingness to think. So let's look at motivation.

Understanding motivation

Instead of revisiting all the old favourites like Maslow, Herzberg and Vroom, think of a time when you were really motivated. The chances are that your motivation was high because you were being stimulated in three interrelated areas:

- You had a strong and pleasurable sense of achievement.
- You had a strong feeling of 'belonging' to a group of people.
- These two areas made you feel good about being you; your self-esteem was high.

What I want you to notice is how much these areas relate to feelings and emotions rather than to logic. Research into neuroscience shows that the brain's limbic system, which governs our feelings, is much more powerful than the neocortex, which controls intellect. In other words, the pathways that have evolved in our brains give emotion priority over logic. The best ever leader you thought of earlier managed to trigger those emotions in you. They did not do that with spreadsheets and computer printouts. They did it by sharing with you their own feelings of purpose, excitement and fulfilment and by making you feel good about 'buying into' that too.

> *'If you really want to motivate someone, go for hearts first and minds second.'*

Organisations are imperfect places, however, so there are often many things to demotivate us, too: for example, company policies and decisions, uncertainty, working environment, unhappy work relationships, excessive workload, being taken for granted and so on. Think about these points, though:

- The really powerful motivators relate to the task, to the people and to an individual's relationship to both.
- The really powerful demotivators relate to the task, to the people and to an individual's relationship to both.
- With the exception of extreme situations such as redundancy, the *leading people* part of your job puts both the powerful motivators and the powerful demotivators in your domain. You can control or, at least, influence them.

Here is another thought on motivation. 'Motivation' is that which causes us to take action. We can, therefore, move along a continuum from demotivation, through grudging acceptance, to logical acceptance, to internalised motivation and, finally, to internalised inspiration. (See the figure opposite.)

Demotivation and its consequences are fairly obvious. If grudging acceptance is sufficient for you to capitalise on performance leverage I will eat my hat. Logical acceptance

Internalised inspiration

Internalised motivation

Logical acceptance

Grudging acceptance

Demotivation

might be enough, but somehow I doubt it, because the source of the motivation is external and far too rational. So unless you have control over bonuses so big you can change people's life-style, logical acceptance is insufficiently powerful to 'make the lever longer'. Internalised motivation means that staff have really bought into what they are doing, and internalised inspiration means they now have the zeal of the converted.

By now you are probably thinking, 'OK, this all makes sense, but what do I actually do?' And there's the rub! If the answer was that simple we would be able to buy it in tablet form to be taken three times a day after meals. What I can do, however, is help point your thinking in the right direction. But you will have to make the decisions yourself. After all, you know yourself and your staff better than I do. Here are four checklists to help you fine-tune your thinking on leadership and motivation.

Your leadership checklist

There is no doubt that leaders are generally charismatic figures who command respect. Charisma and respect, however, are not something leaders have: they are things that people feel about leaders. They are determined by what the leaders do. This checklist, therefore, will help you focus on leadership qualities, abilities and attitudes and translate them into actions. (See pages 50–2).

It outlines the actions associated with the four qualities of vision, integrity, determination and believability, the two abilities of technical/managerial competence and inter-personal skills, and the three attitudes of being people-oriented, thinking positively and walking the talk. Here are some details about them. As you read them, resist the temptation to define quality, ability and attitude and instead focus on what it is leaders actually do. Then you can complete the Leadership checklist.

| Vision | Managers maintain things, leaders change things. They have to be able to see in their mind's eye how they want things to be. Your goal might be much less ambitious than starting a new religion, saving a rainforest or invading Poland but you have to be able to see it in your mind's eye in sufficient detail to visualise what people are saying, doing and feeling. You can bring the corporate mission to fruition at the point of customer contact, for example, only if you can see in your mind's eye what people will say, do and feel when they are face to face with customers. This is the kind of detail you need to go into. Most organisations' vision and values statements just do not go into sufficient detail. Few things have happened as a result of human intervention without first existing in someone's mind's eye. So, even if you have to begin with a little daydreaming, it is essential that your visualisation goes from wishes to goals to feelings to observations. Can you see in your mind's eye what you |

Vision	want your staff to do, think and feel in relation to your goals?
Integrity	Consistency, openness, honesty and respect for people are essential if you want them to follow you. Could someone tell from how you spend your time what your vision is?
Determination	Leaders encounter more obstacles changing things than managers encounter maintaining things but they do not give up. They are so determined they persevere. How determined are you to achieve your goal? Less than 100 per cent may not be enough.
Believability	Integrity and determination combine with interpersonal skills to add to a leader's believability. Whether you are a Viking raider or a telephone sales clerk, faith in your leader is essential to your motivation. Another ingredient is enthusiasm. If you are not enthusiastic about your vision and your people, no one will believe in you. Do your staff believe in you?
Technical and managerial competence	You do not have to be the best technician or manager to be a credible leader, but you need to be good enough to avoid making a fool of yourself and losing too much time doing things and managing processes. You need to spend a good chunk of your time (some say as much as 20 per cent) taking action to support your vision and values.
Interpersonal skills	Inspiring people to buy into your vision is unlikely to be achievable by e-mail. You will have to talk to people. You may not be addressing the Nuremberg Rally or delivering the Sermon on the Mount, but you will have to build rapport with people, influence them and sometimes be assertive with them. It is no coincidence that leaders have above-average interpersonal skills. When did you last assess your interpersonal skills or attend an interpersonal skills course?
People-oriented	Can you imagine a carpenter who does not like wood, a vet who does not like animals or a schoolteacher who does not like children *and* who is good at their job? By the same token, can you imagine a leader who does not like people? After all, people are a leader's raw material. That is why effective leaders enjoy being with people, working with them and developing them. How people-oriented are you?

Positive thinking	Leaders encounter obstacles. Positive thinking is the starting point of the determination that carries leaders through, over and around them. Attitudes are contagious. The more positive you are, the more your staff overcome obstacles, display a 'can do' attitude and spot opportunities. Are you a positive thinker? When did you last read a positive thinking book, listen to a positive thinking audio tape or attend a positive thinking course?
Walking the talk	Walking the talk is an important part of integrity. People can see you mean what you say and that you apply it to yourself.

Your leadership checklist

			Priority
I have neither a vision nor long-term goals, or, if I do have any, I keep them to myself.	**Quality – Vision** ☐ ☐ ☐ ☐ ☐	I can see clearly in my mind's eye how things will be different and how people will feel as a result of being part of this process.	
I am inconsistent in my actions. People cannot tell from my behaviour what is important to me. I tend not to trust my staff.	**Quality – Integrity** ☐ ☐ ☐ ☐ ☐	My actions are totally consistent with my vision; they are consistent over time; my actions display my honesty and genuine respect for my staff.	
My enthusiasm peters out. I find it hard to maintain focus. Obstacles throw me.	**Quality – Determination** ☐ ☐ ☐ ☐ ☐	My staff know that obstacles are stepping stones that take us nearer to our vision. I never compromise on essentials.	

I lack the courage of my convictions. I feel we are unlikely to achieve what we need to achieve. People can tell that from the way I communicate.	**Quality – Believability** ☐ ☐ ☐ ☐ ☐	Even though my vision is a bold one, people believe me when I say we'll do it; they believe we can succeed because of me.	
I lack the technical and management competence for my job. My time management is poor. I am not good at managing my staff's performance.	**Ability – Technical and managerial competence** ☐ ☐ ☐ ☐ ☐	Whether or not I am the best, staff respect my technical ability, my ability to manage my time and the way I manage their performance.	
I am not comfortable addressing staff. I do not chair meetings very well. I am either aggressive or submissive. Listening is not a strength.	**Ability – Interpersonal skills** ☐ ☐ ☐ ☐ ☐	I am very comfortable addressing staff. I chair meetings well. I am assertive. I listen very well. I can influence and coach.	
I am not really a people person. I expect others to inconvenience themselves for me. My staff sink or swim by their own merits. They are my resource to help me get my job done.	**Attitude – people** ☐ ☐ ☐ ☐ ☐	I like people and seek out their company. People come first; I often inconvenience myself for others. I support my staff; I am there to help them.	

I can be prone to mood swings. I see obstacles where others don't. I have a moan now and then.	**Attitude – positive thinking** ☐ ☐ ☐ ☐ ☐	I am consistently positive. Obstacles and mistakes have benefits. I help others see the positive side. I listen to grievances but do not tolerate moaning.	
Staff might accuse me of saying and doing different things or being guilty of 'Do as I say, not as I do'.	**Attitude – Walking the talk** ☐ ☐ ☐ ☐ ☐	I have identified the behaviours from staff essential for my vision and I deliberately ensure they are visible in my own behaviours.	

Your 'walking the talk' checklist

Credible leaders walk the talk. They display in their behaviour the behaviours they need to see from others to achieve their vision. As I do not know what behaviours you need your staff to display I have provided a list of suggestions below. It will be of most benefit if you tick the behaviours you need to see, then assess the extent to which you exhibit them yourself and, finally, identify priorities for action.

Your 'ideas that motivate' checklist

One of the commonest questions I am asked on leadership courses is 'How do I motivate my staff?' as if there was

Behaviour	✓	My score 1 to 10	Priority for action
Displays buy-in to vision, goals			
Has high technical skills			
Has high performance expectations			
Is hardworking; goes the extra mile			
Is conscientious			
Is reliable; sticks to deadlines, appointments			
Displays good time management			
Develops own skills and/or those of others			
Supports other team members; helps others meet deadlines			
Helps maintain team cohesion, morale and focus			
Helps people 'upstream' and 'downstream' in the process			
Accepts responsibility, owns problems, is solution-oriented			
Sees the bigger picture			
Pre-empts problems			
Displays initiative and/or creativity			
Focuses on goal achievement			
Is customer-focused			
Has positive attitude			
Is people-oriented; listens; gives time to others; keeps promises; demonstrates respect for others			
Is honest, open, shares information freely			
Networks; builds constructive alliances			
Laughs and has fun at appropriate times; brightens the atmosphere			

some kind of easy answer. In answering the question, there is very little between the extremes of responding with general principles and of listing specific examples of what some managers find effective in their particular situation. So here are some general principles followed by a list of specific ideas. If none of the ideas appeals to you, consider whether any would appeal to your staff. (After all, they are not you.) Failing that, perhaps you can think of a few from your own experience. If you are unsure as to the purpose of these ideas, remember that grudging acceptance of goals is unlikely to be sufficient to encourage the level of performance you need.

General principles
There are a few key rules to remember when adopting motivational ideas.

Different strokes for different folks. What motivates one person may not motivate another. A nuclear research physicist, for example, is likely to be motivated by the content of the job. An operative on a supermarket checkout will probably gain more satisfaction from team feeling. The scientist's self-esteem might need accolades from fellow scientists while the supermarket operative's self-esteem might be triggered by good feedback from a customer.

Internal motivation is more effective than external motivation. Hence we need appropriate strokes for the folks, and those strokes have to be delivered appropriately. That way, the motivational activities have impact at an emotional level and staff internalise the motivation.

Perception is important. I once had a meeting with the European president of a medium-sized company. Reception told me I could find him in the kitchen. In addition to a sink and cupboards, the kitchen contained several large round tables, presumably where staff had lunch. Around one of the tables was a group of people drinking coffee, eating croissants and opening mail. One of them was the president. I asked him later what they were doing. He said, 'We're too small to employ someone just to do the mail, so it always fell to the most junior person, and soon a stigma got attached to it. Everyone who had to do it resented it. It became a source of demotivation. So now we do it on a team rota with coffee and croissants. It's a bit like an early morning party. Opening the post has gone from being a chore to being fun.'

You have to get the basics right first. All the externally applied motivational activities in the world will not make up for poor management, taking staff for granted, treating them with disrespect and so on.

Motivating ideas
Having established these ground rules, here is a selection of ideas. Their purpose is to trigger your thinking:

1 Take action to remove demotivators. This will release the handbrake, as it were. (If you don't know what demotivates your staff, ask them – and then listen.)
2 Address all aspects of underperformance swiftly, respectfully and exactly as laid out in organisational procedures.

3 Smile more; put more energy into your walk; let staff see your enthusiasm for performance and for them as people; encourage laughter and laugh out loud more yourself. (Ask yourself this telling question, 'If your staff were laughing when you walked into the room, would they stop laughing or would they share the joke with you?')

4 Find out what your staff feel (really feel) about you, each other, the job and so on. If you don't know, you are too distant from them.

5 Show you trust staff by making them accountable, with appropriate training and support, for something worthwhile. If this initially makes you feel uncomfortable, accept that discomfort as part of your own development process. It is only a temporary feeling.

6 Link each individual's personal development to key areas of performance and to personal goals. Walk the talk by doing the same for yourself.

7 Ensure that all performance measures are clear, fair and accepted by staff.

8 Put up a whiteboard where the team can see it for jokes, cartoons, good ideas, welcomes, farewells, requests for help and so on. Clear it every two weeks. If your staff are geographically dispersed, use a computer bulletin board instead.

9 Turn a learning event into both fun and a social activity – for example, hold a trivia quiz on essential knowledge.

10 Turn more experienced staff into trainers, coaches or mentors of less experienced staff.

11 Celebrate performance achievements and personal

achievements (both inside and outside work) in a way that provides positive strokes.

12 Instigate performance-based fun competition between teams (with the emphasis on fun).

13 Get staff who attend a training course or conference to lead a session on their return, sharing what they have learned with the rest of the team.

14 Share and explain organisational/section goals and values, and jointly plan how you will implement them.

15 Increase communication between you and your staff, especially on matters of organisational change and on matters affecting them.

16 Make it normal and safe for your staff to give you ideas, complaints, feedback, feelings and so on.

17 Share your mistakes with staff (and what you learned from them).

18 Treat mistakes staff make as learning opportunities. Coach them into rectifying the problem and learning from it. (One of the things they should learn as a result of your interaction is that you are there to help them.)

19 Ask the team regularly, 'To help you perform better and enjoy work more, what do you want me to do more of and what do you want me to do less of?'

20 Ask the team to answer the same question about each other.

21 Give frequent and regular feedback on individual and team performance.

22 Seek, listen to and act on feedback from staff on your performance as their leader.

23 Critically assess the respect you show to staff.

24 Put your staff first.
25 Tackle unpleasant jobs yourself before delegating them to staff.
26 If there is a task that no one wants to do, join in and turn it into a treat or a bit of fun.
27 Communicate bad news or reprimands face to face, never by memo or e-mail.
28 Critically assess your enthusiasm for your work, your goals and your team. You can't afford less than 10/10.
29 Remove trappings of your own status and make your staff the heroes.
30 Focus hard on performance in the team's key areas and don't nit-pick peripheral matters. Be tough on performance, yet helpful and supportive to people.
31 Spend time with staff as a group and as individuals. Never rush conversations with staff.
32 Ditch open-door policies in favour of MBWA (Managing By Wandering Around – observing, listening, helping and praising as you do so).
33 Spend a significant amount of time coaching staff.
34 Link hard work and success to fun; reward effort as well as results. You can use smiles, praise, presents or social activities – as long as the team feels they are appropriate and fair.
35 Invite a more senior manager into the next team meeting to congratulate staff on their success.
36 Invite a customer (internal or external) into the next team meeting to discuss how you can all help one another perform better.
37 Collect and distribute details of what staff have done to satisfy customers.
38 Encourage out-of-work social activities that the team

will enjoy. Whether it is a night at the opera, a quick beer, paint-balling or fell-walking, attendance must be voluntary.

39 Spend ten minutes 'chilling out' with the team over coffee, croissants, doughnuts or biscuits.

40 Introduce tea, coffee, croissants, doughnuts or biscuits to team meetings.

41 Display (and change regularly) pictures of staff at work, satisfying customers, on team social activities and so on. Choose pictures that show everyone having fun.

42 Encourage the team to adopt a charity and undertake fund-raising activities. Turn the activities and the hand-over of raised funds into team events – letting them take the credit.

43 Use small but genuine gestures of appreciation – for example, praise a staff member to a more senior person (in front of the staff member), send a personally penned 'Thank you' note or distribute customer praise.

44 Seek opportunities to help staff perform better and develop their careers. Assist ambitious and talented staff to develop, grow and move on.

45 Set yourself a personal daily target to make at least one team member smile, make another laugh, make another feel good about themselves and their performance, make another realise what they have just learned and another to feel glad you are their manager.

> *Effective motivation is rarely rational; it hits you at an emotional level!*

10 ways to kill inner motivation stone dead and make your job more difficult

1 Think that management is about control and behave as if you can control your staff into high performance.
2 Act on the basis that your staff are your resource to help you achieve your targets.
3 Act on the basis that your staff are inferior to you.
4 Assume your staff are motivated only by money while you, of course, are motivated by more socially acceptable qualities.
5 Insult your staff by offering paltry financial incentives to achieve something.
6 Have favourites; be biased.
7 Bully, shout at, manipulate or victimise staff; make them feel guilty, anxious or vulnerable.
8 Keep staff in the dark, treating them like mushrooms; assume they are telepathic; assume they are not interested in 'management' matters or important issues.
9 Use criticism rather than praise to modify staff behaviour.
10 Present one face to staff and another to more senior management.

Teams and teambuilding

Teamwork is becoming increasingly important. As organisations have downsized and introduced empowerment, more people have to work interdependently with others to achieve a goal. Sometimes the team consists of your immediate work colleagues. Sometimes your teammates are people from adjacent departments. Increasingly, as initiatives like value chain management are implemented, they are people from other organisations. Sometimes, in virtual teams, we do not even get to meet our team-mates face to face. Teamwork is on the increase. The person who transforms a group of people into a cohesive, interdependently working team is, of course, the leader.

So how do you know if you are building a team effectively? Look at the list on page 62, where you will find the characteristics of effective and ineffective teams.

Based on these characteristics, how would you describe your team? Is that how you would like to describe it? You may be wondering what you can do to encourage teamwork and team spirit. First, it is a good idea to remember that human beings are gregarious by nature. We have a strong need to belong to a group. Second, teamwork can be a product of rational thinking, but team spirit is a product of emotional thinking. You need, therefore, to address both the rational and emotional sides of people's brains. Here are some suggestions:

- Explain the team's purpose in relation to the organisation or the team's customers, not just in terms of the team's operational processes.
- Ensure acceptance of purpose and goals by employing the appropriate leadership style.
- Vary your style according to the cohesion of the team and team-members' acceptance of team goals. Ensure they have the right balance between support and autonomy.

Ineffective	Effective
■ No sense of purpose or obvious commitment to one	■ Sense of purpose to which everyone is committed
■ Successes not celebrated; feedback mostly negative	■ Successes celebrated; team feels good about achievements
■ People are cautious, holding back contributions and ideas; they moan frequently; they dwell on problems	■ Individual roles and goals are clear
■ New ideas are resisted	■ Feedback is constructive
■ Team is insulated from outside; inconvenient feedback is 'rationalised' away; outsiders are stereotyped; there is pressure to conform to negative values	■ People feel safe to say and think what they feel; contributions are valued; there is mutual support
■ Frustration and lethargy.	■ People discuss the way the team is working; it is solution-oriented; new ideas are welcomed; change is assessed positively; there is encouragement to conform to positive values
	■ General feeling of progress, togetherness and fun.

- ■ Involve the whole team in planning the steps needed to achieve goals.
- ■ Ensure that working conditions and resources are appropriate.
- ■ Ensure that the team has relevant and timely information.

- Spend time with individual team-members, explaining their responsibilities, performance standards and authority, and coaching them.
- Agree with the team how members will monitor their own performance.
- Agree with the team the level and type of help they need from you to achieve goals.
- Ensure the size and make-up of the team is appropriate.
- Facilitate team spirit.
- Represent the team.
- Manage the boundary and handle 'interference' for them.
- Tackle outside interference.
- Spend time with the team. Create opportunities for them to experience 'togetherness' and fun.
- Celebrate team and individual success and special occasions.
- Induct new members thoroughly, agreeing individual roles, targets and so on. Ensure that an experienced team-member looks after new team-members while they settle in.
- Monitor individual performance and give constructive feedback.
- Address poor performance quickly and constructively.
- Support individuals with problems.
- Be a good role model. Be enthusiastic and optimistic about the purpose and goals.

Teams are like plants: they need nourishment to thrive. They need to:

- understand the context in which they operate
- understand their purpose and goals
- receive constructive feedback
- receive relevant and timely information
- experience the right balance between support and autonomy
- feel confident that their team leader is managing the boundary between them and other teams
- experience 'togetherness' and fun.

Think of your own team and ask how they would score on each of these items. Think also of how deliberately you address them. The list of 45 motivating ideas above contains several ideas that can enhance teamwork and team feeling. To help you further, the table on page 68 contains a list of actions. As you read it, identify the ones with most potential for your team.

'Consulting with and involving staff as a team is vital.'

Your top 10 tips

As I said at the beginning of this chapter, leadership is a much studied and little understood subject. Breaking it down can help us understand it better, but it only works when it comes together. As with the recipe for a meal, ingredients and actions have to come together to form a coherent whole. They also need to be appropriate to the purpose. In the same way that a favourite children's meal would be inappropriate for a formal dinner, so the leadership actions appropriate in a crisis could backfire alarmingly in other situations. That is why, in this chapter, I have tried to help your understanding of the subject so that you can make sensible decisions appropriate to each situation.

By way of summary, however, and to stimulate your thoughts still further, here are my top 10 tips for developing as a leader.

1 *Develop an insatiable curiosity.* The future belongs to those people who see ideas and trends before they become obvious. The only way you can do that is to soak up information from as great a variety of sources as possible. So listen to people you would not normally speak to, read some magazines you would not normally buy, go to places you would not normally visit. It will help you see 'over the horizon' and will help generate ideas.

2 *Learn about and practise creative thinking.* At one time the past was a reasonable guide to the future. Not any more. In fact, the future will never be the same again! Being creative will help you work smarter, 'stay ahead' and be positive in the face of obstacles.

3 *Daydream.* Work on your mind's eye view of how you want things to be. Take it to the level of detail where you can hear what people are saying and experience what they are feeling. That is your vision.

4 *Identify the stepping-stones that will get you there.* You may believe passionately in your vision, but without a plan you will never achieve it. A plan (even a wild one) is part of your believability.

5 *Remember that, as a leader, you're there to change things, not to maintain things. But you can't do it alone.* Your team can achieve goals without you but you can't achieve much

without them. In effect, you need them more than they need you. Turn your people into heroes. Let them take the glory. In many respects, the leader's role is a humble one.

6 *Remember, they are the 'players on the pitch'.* The 'people' part of your job is to give them the ability, desire, opportunity and confidence to perform well. Ask yourself, are you the 'performance police officer' or the 'performance coach'?

7 *Think holistically about performance.* Be clear in your own mind about the performance and behaviour you want from your team and the performance and behaviour you don't want. Communicate that difference in as motivating a way as possible because really good performance cannot be obtained by order or compulsion. Ignore the false boundary between working and learning. Become the team coach and turn working into motivational learning.

8 *Think culture, culture, culture in all your interaction with staff.* Remember that you set an example whether you mean to or not, so walk the talk. Be consistent. Be honest. Never assume that problems will blow over or sort themselves out. Be proactive. Address problems while they are small enough to be nipped in the bud. Catch people doing something right – it is a more effective method of communication than always catching them doing something wrong. Listen to people when they talk to you. Listen to gossip. Listen to the grapevine. Encourage staff to express their opinions especially when they differ from yours. Remember, we have two eyes, two ears and one mouth. Effective leaders use them in that ratio.

9 *Don't confuse respect with fear, 'distance' or status.* Respect is something staff can only give you of their own free will. It has nothing to do with your position in the hierarchy, experience or professional qualifications. It has everything to do with how you interact with them. Treat all staff with respect in all you do and their respect for you will come as a natural consequence.

10 *Do at least one thing each day to give someone a feeling of uplift and confidence.* How people feel about us is dependent on how we make them feel about themselves. This tip is the quickest way to stimulate their motivation, encourage them to buy into goals and give you their respect.

> *Good leaders know what norms and values will contribute to high performance and reinforce them in their daily interactions with staff.*

Actions to help teamwork and team feeling
1	Discussing the purpose and goal of new initiatives with team, and involving them in planning how to achieve them
2	Discussing individuals' goals, responsibilities, work standards and authority
3	Agreeing with the team how they would like to monitor performance and progress, and how they would like you to help them
4	Ensuring the size and make-up of the team are appropriate, including getting poor performers back on track or removing them fairly, supportively and in accordance with procedures
5	Tackling anything that interferes with team effectiveness
6	Going out of your way to ensure that working conditions and resources are the best for the job
7	Inducting new members thoroughly, participating in some of their induction personally
8	Spending time with the team
9	Celebrating team success and individual success
10	Initiating actions to facilitate team spirit
11	Supporting individuals with problems
12	Being a good role model

4

Moments of truth

Acknowledging the three parts of your job – doing things, managing processes and leading people – helps you understand more about leadership. What I have not mentioned so far, however, is that they are not always mutually exclusive. You are unlikely to schedule your day, for example, by saying, 'Right, I'll manage processes until lunchtime and then go and lead some people.' They are often inextricably intertwined. That is why, in this section, I am going to show you how to handle the numerous 'intertwined' incidents when your leadership credibility is on the line. I call those incidents 'moments of truth'. The term 'moment of truth' is mostly used in customer care. Understanding how it is used in that context will help you understand its relevance to leadership.

Moments of truth

The term is most associated with Jan Carlsen, a former chief executive of the Scandinavian Air Services (SAS) and one of the 'founding fathers' of customer care. Taking over the airline in the depths of a recession he knew he had to make a difference quickly and applied a simple logic – 'We have the same aircraft and the same routes as other airlines. The only thing that differentiates us from our competitors is our people.' He estimated that, on average, a passenger would come into contact with a member of SAS staff five times a trip and that each of those five contacts was a defining moment – a moment of truth – because it was in that moment that the customer would decide whether or not SAS was the airline to fly with. So all they had to do was to manage the dickens out of those few, brief customer interactions. The approach was both incisive and successful.

The moments of truth concept is so useful to customer care because suppliers tend to see their jobs as one long continuum, from A to Z as it were. Customers, on the other hand, see only a few sporadic 'snapshots' of interaction. Take, for example, the supermarket where you shop. The staff employed there probably see their jobs from the start of a shift to the end of a shift as one long continuum. What do you see? A couple of brief 'snapshots' of interaction. Despite the large number of hours the supermarket staff spend at work, your impression of the supermarket is determined by the response you get from a shelf-stacker when you ask where the baked beans are and the greeting you get from the checkout operator.

Understanding moments of truth helps the supermarket staff see the supplier/customer interaction from your viewpoint. It enables them to manage the dickens out of those few brief but critical interactions.

Similarly, you know you job from A to Z: from the moment you get into work to the moment you go home. All your staff see, however, is a few 'snapshots' of interaction. It is during those brief 'snapshot' interactions that your leadership credibility is on the line.

Leadership moments of truth can be many and varied. They can range from greeting staff in the morning to running a team meeting to addressing a problem to giving feedback to passing staff in a corridor.

Trying to describe how to handle every single moment of truth you might encounter would be a formidable and overly prescriptive task. What I can do, however, is give you some guidance on the skills and thinking that will enable you to handle moments of truth positively. I have provided that guidance alphabetically to make it easy for you to dip into it according to your needs and interests. The list covers:

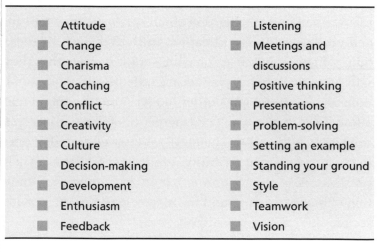

Attitude	Listening
Change	Meetings and
Charisma	discussions
Coaching	Positive thinking
Conflict	Presentations
Creativity	Problem-solving
Culture	Setting an example
Decision-making	Standing your ground
Development	Style
Enthusiasm	Teamwork
Feedback	Vision

Note. Where a topic has been covered earlier in the book, I have referred you to the relevant section.

Attitude

The way most of us think is a product of our culture, and our culture has its roots in history. To explain a modern leadership mindset, therefore, I will have to go back into recent history.

Until fairly recently, our major wealth producers were manufacturing organisations, for which competitive advantage hinged on the relationship between market share, price and economies of scale. Output came from a deskilled, production-line workforce with limited education and minimal expectations of job satisfaction. 'Managing' was a mix of organising workflow and controlling workers.

Then, as a result of serious competition from emerging nations, most notably in the Far East, we began to realise that we had to do something about quality, customer care and processes. As I said earlier, initiatives such as these do not happen because someone senior decrees that they will happen; they happen because the people who at one time were thought of as order fodder 'buy into them' and allow them to happen. The emergence of these initiatives coincided with other changes: a better-educated workforce, greater social mobility, higher expectations of job satisfaction, a mushrooming use of technology, contraction of manufacturing and the meteoric rise of the service sector.

Increasingly, competitive advantage lies in niche marketing, added value, excellent quality and superior service. Consequently, not only do more people earn their living using their brains more than their hands, their emotional 'buy-in' to what they do is as crucial to organisational success as marketing and cost control.

Those organisations that successfully made the shift from 'old economy' to 'new economy' did so because of strong leadership from the top. These leaders had to battle against the vested interests of, on the one hand, traditional trade unions and, on the other, an army of middle managers with substantial vested interests in the 'old economy'. Many of these leaders were charismatic figures who have greatly influenced leadership thinking but, and this is a big but, because of the size of the challenges they faced, their position at the head of the organisation and the publicity they attracted, they are still the corporate equivalent of military generals rousing their mass troops for battle.

The world is different now. The changes I referred to above are no longer novel. They are commonplace. A whole generation has grown up in the workplace knowing nothing different. What really affects organisational performance now, however, is individual employees' ability and willingness to 'connect' emotionally to organisational goals. And the biggest single influence on that ability and willingness is their immediate line manager. Consequently, the leading-people part of every manager's job has become much more significant.

Managers who accept the leading people part of their job reluctantly will never do it that well. Staff have an incredibly sensitive b******t monitor and will see through reluctant actions. If you refer back to the information in the Introduction (see page xvii) on leadership leverage, however, you will soon see that capitalising on the *leading-people* part of your job benefits you, because your perform-ance is little other than the sum total of the performance of your people. The better they perform, the more favourably it reflects on you.

You will also find that your job becomes easier and more rewarding: 'easier' because enthusiastic staff with a clear sense of direction require less energy-sapping and time-consuming supervision; 'rewarding' because you will be positively enhancing the lives of fellow human beings. You do not have to wait for heaven to enjoy the benefits of that.

Change

Change is such a ubiquitous feature of organisational life that most managers need the ability to handle it. How you handle change has a significant effect on both the success of the change and on your credibility as a leader. An important ingredient of implementing change is knowing what to communicate to whom and how to communicate it.

In most change situations, some people will 'lose' and some people will 'gain'. Those who gain (the 'winners') will be more enthusiastic about the change than those people who feel they are losing something. The word 'feel' is important, because people's *perceptions* of what they gain or lose determine how they react. Managing change successfully, therefore, means using communica-tion to affect those perceptions.

Part of your preparation is to 'read' the situation, identify those people who feel they will 'win' and those who feel they will 'lose' and determine an appropriate strategy to affect their perceptions. An additional feature of your preparation is to consider the ability of the 'winners' and 'losers' to affect the change. Where 'winners' have power to influence others, the proposed change has a better chance of success. Where 'losers' have power to influence others, the proposed change can run into problems.

By using the 'winners/losers' matrix overleaf to analyse the situation, you will begin to see whom you have to influence. Basically, you need to move people in the direction of the solid arrows (preferably) or dashed arrows (second choice). Here is an example of how easily, by using effective communication, you can change perceptions of 'winning' and 'losing'. I was once involved with a bank in an offshore financial centre that was amalgamating with another bank and relocating to a new office for the amalgamated bank. The big problem was that people did not know what they did not know. Consequently, rumours were running rife and morale was suffering. The senior manager responsible for the change process attended a creative thinking course I ran on the island and one of the ideas generated during the course was to install a telephone hot-line so that staff with queries could get through to him directly. It was red hot for a couple of days and then hardly rang at all. Its mere presence reassured staff that they had no need to worry about what they did not know. Their 'loser' perception had been altered.

Perceptions can often be altered by giving people full and timely communication, by listening to and acting on their

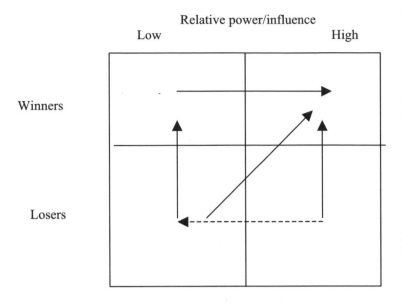

In times of change, use effective communication to help people realise how they will benefit (solid arrows) or to lessen the negative influence of those who feel they may lose out (dashed arrow).

concerns, by selling ideas to them rather than just telling them what will happen and by involving them during the formative stages of the change. Remember the golden rule: issues are resolved faster and stay resolved longer when those affected play an active part in reaching the solution.

Charisma

I think most of us would have difficulty defining charisma – yet we seem to recognise it easily enough when we see it. We also know it is something leaders tend to possess.

We feel someone has charisma when we see a special talent or quality that we admire. As the word 'charisma' has its roots in the ancient Greek word for 'a God-given gift', I would not like to suggest that my offering is in the same category. Admirable talents or qualities, however, can be analysed, understood and emulated. So here is some information from a variety of disciplines that could be seen as 'special' by other people. As you read it, please remember that our feelings towards another person are usually the result of a whole cluster of factors. None of the following suggestions on its own is likely to make much difference. When applied along with other suggestions in this moments-of-truth section, however, it will all add up.

Appearance. A substantial amount of information reaches our brains visually, and much visual information reaches our brains subconsciously. We do not know it has arrived, we just know we have a feeling about what we have seen. This means that people gain an impression about us very quickly. You can help people gain the 'right' impression about you by looking the part. In other words, by ensuring that your appearance is positive, both you and others can feel you are an effective leader.

Speech. The words you use can have a significant effect on the impression you make if you choose them wisely, especially when addressing groups. The numbers you address might be more modest than those attending the Nuremberg Rally or those listening to the Sermon on the Mount, but research from a variety of sources provides food for thought. According to research from Roffey Park Management College, leaders often use an 'I...we...' speech pattern. For example, 'I believe that customers are crucial so we all need to check that we're exceeding their expectations.' Or 'I feel that there is untapped potential in everyone, so I would like us all to review what we're doing to develop our staff.' The 'I' part of this speech pattern says that you are a free-thinking, assertive visionary and the 'we' part says that you are a leader/team worker – not a bad combination in one sentence.

According to research from King's College, London, successful speakers generate positive feelings in an audience by packaging their message in a non-offensive way, often using humour, analogies and metaphors to make their point. According to research published in the *Harvard Business Review*, powerful communicators use image-based words. By way of example, a 'new path' has more impact than an 'alternative', 'exploring' is more proactive than 'inquiring' and Martin Luther King's 'I have a dream' would not have had the same impact had he only had 'a good idea'.

Personal touch. Another important quality we admire in leaders is the personal touch. It can best be described as a kind of 'personal connection' between two people. Important elements of that connection are:

- *Eye contact* – because this is how we let other people know that we acknowledge their presence and that they have our attention. While important throughout a conversation, it is doubly important at the beginning and end of a conversation.
- *A genuine smile* – because that is how we show other people we are pleased to see them. Again,

it is doubly important at the beginning and end of a conversation.

- *Addressing people by name* – because that is a powerful positive stroke. Remembering people's names is easier if, as you are introduced to them, you repeat it at least three times to yourself while you are looking at them. (If you are thinking, 'How do I do that while I'm talking?' see the next point.)
- *Rapport* – the feeling of 'comfort' with someone else. We feel as if we and the other people are 'on the same wavelength'. You can deliberately speed up the rapport-building process by consciously practising three behaviours. First, make your posture similar to the other person's. Second, borrow some of the other people's terminology when you respond to them. These actions should be subtle. If the other people consciously notice you doing them, the effect will be lost and the actions will probably even irritate your listeners. Third, show genuine interest in them. Find out something about them. Probe to show you are interested. Listen to them. (While a person is talking you can be memorising his or her name.) Not only is showing interest in someone another powerful positive stroke, you can then follow up the conversation next time you see them – for example 'Last time we met you were just about to go on holiday. How was it?' This takes very little effort and has a hugely disproportionate positive effect.

- *Relaxation* – do not just be relaxed yourself; help others relax with you by incorporating all the points mentioned above in your interaction. Your aim is to make people feel good interacting with you.
- *Mixing with people* – there is something special about being with people on their terms. They will talk to you in a way that they never would do otherwise. They also get to know you in a way that they never would do otherwise. To mix with people, you may try MBWA ('managing by wandering around' listening to people) popularised by Tom Peters in *In Search of Excellence*, regularly lunching in the staff restaurant as Sir John Egan did when he was saving Jaguar Cars, or the equivalent of sleeping with the troops under tanks in the desert as Sir Peter de la Billière did during the Gulf War. Whatever you do, the trick is to do it genuinely, do it regularly, share the same conditions as everyone else and listen openly.

Coaching

Coaching is a vital and beneficial skill. Coaching delivers better-performing staff, staff who think more and staff who relate to you better. Unfortunately, it rarely comes naturally to us. You can find detailed guidance on coaching in Chapter 2, Developing performance potential.

Conflict

Organisations exist in a state of dynamic tension. One person's good idea can be another's headache; one person's initiative can mean extra work for someone else; one person's deadline can be someone else's priority clash. Consequently, you can spend a lot of time trying to resolve conflict.

As a leader, you will often be the one called upon to resolve conflict between your team and other managers' teams and between members of your own team. How you handle such situations will affect your credibility as a leader. Handling conflict is easier if you appreciate:

- the main characteristics of conflict situations
- the advantages and disadvantages of handling such situations in particular ways
- the behaviours that help you and the other person reach a satisfactory solution.

The main characteristics of conflict situations are that one or both parties allow their emotions to run high, refuse to compromise, refuse to acknowledge that the other person's point is valid, present opinions as if they were facts, belittle the other person and his or her viewpoint, interrupt and disagree. It is little wonder, therefore, that not many of us relish such situations and sometimes handle them negatively.

Fear of conflict can lead us to deny the problem exists or to ignore it, hoping it will right itself. While this approach enables us to avoid confrontation and any negative repercussions that addressing the issue might cause, the problem is usually only deferred and can become even more difficult to resolve the longer it is left. The deferment can also affect your credibility, self-esteem and stress levels and your relationship with the people involved. Sometimes we minimise the problem, placating the other person, or we address the symptoms rather than the cause. This leaves you in the same position as that described above. Alternatively, you can address the problem, tackle it deliberately and seek a satisfactory resolution. As long as you have the appropriate skills, the problem is solved sooner, your credibility improves and, usually, so does the relationship between the parties.

Handling conflict requires the following skills or attributes:

- the ability to remain calm (or, at least, appear calm), use neutral body language and maintain good eye contact
- the ability to keep the confrontation (and any exaggeration, generalisations and belittling remarks) in perspective and keep the overall goal in sight
- frequently, a degree of creativity to find novel solutions attractive to all parties
- genuine listening skills.

This last point warrants special attention. Emotions can run very high in conflicts. People in conflict will probably exaggerate, appear very stubborn and, in the belief that it will strengthen their case, present what they say in very strong terms. If you listen, probe and try hard to understand them without trying to counter their arguments at this stage, you will find that when you do present your side:

- you have had the benefit of more thinking time
- they are more likely to listen to you because you have just listened to them
- you know how to tailor what you say to be more acceptable to them
- they feel better about the process and the outcome.

Make no mistake about it, though, it can require a great deal of self-discipline to listen genuinely to the other people's arguments, assumptions, beliefs and points of view. But doing so gives you a head start over less patient people and dramatically improves your chances of resolving the conflict – and that, in turn, adds to your leadership credibility.

> *Effective leaders have two eyes, two ears and one mouth. When resolving conflict they use them in that ratio.*

Creativity

We expect leaders to overcome obstacles and to find better ways of achieving goals. You may do this yourself, say, in response to a crisis, or encourage others to overcome obstacles and find better ways to achieve goals as part of the 'climate' and empowerment you create. We need more creativity because of the pace of change.

Traditional approaches to problems and decisions emphasise people's ability to analyse past situations and predict the future. That used to be satisfactory, because the past was once an adequate guide to the future. Increasingly, however, in today's high-velocity, extremely competitive situations, we need to think of new ways of tackling new challenges. So being creative is essential for task achievement and for your credibility as a leader. It will also enable you to set the right example and coach your people more effectively.

Thinking creatively begins with recognising the difference between convergent thinking and divergent thinking. Convergent thinking means narrowing down your options in response to a problem until you reach a conclusion. Divergent thinking means expanding your options in response to a situation so that you have a choice of options, many of which have never been considered before. Our society, however, is more geared towards convergent thinking.

Western society tends to prize rational thinking more highly than creative thinking. To pass most school exams and to receive good appraisals at work you need to be rational rather then creative. The average creative person (in the arts) earns much less than the average rational person (in other occupations). Consequently, we gain more practice at rational thinking than we do at creative thinking. One study of US and Canadian companies found that in 60 per cent of cases there was little attempt to explore options. Most options were identified by copying what other firms did. If you adopt that approach, the most you can hope for is being 'No worse than anyone else'.

> *Creativity is the only way to break out of the trap of rational incrementalism and achieve breakthrough results.*

Have you ever wondered how creative you are? Here are some thoughts that might help you answer that question:

1 Are you comfortable being seen as different from others?
2 To what extent did your upbringing encourage you to be creative?
3 How comfortable are you with ambiguity and disorder?
4 How enthusiastic are you about new places and new acquaintances?
5 To what extent do you enjoy daydreaming and believe it to be worthwhile?
6 To what extent do you rely on your feelings, intuition and gut reaction?
7 To what extent are you reactive rather than proactive?
8 How far ahead do you look?
9 Would people describe you as 'innovative'?
10 How many examples can you cite of your creative approach to problems?

Most of us need help to think creatively. That help comes in the shape of lateral thinking techniques – techniques to help us avoid the rut of convergent thinking and leap sideways in alternate thinking directions.

There are many lateral thinking techniques, but here are the ones I find managers are most comfortable with.

   ▪ *Restating the problem* – this is not only a useful technique in its own right, it is an essential beginning to all the other techniques. Several of the ways in which you can restate the problem are shown in the table on page 88.

- *Why and how questions* – here is an example. Let's say you believe your company needs more graduate trainees. After all, we know that talented people are scarce and many companies have a history of recruiting graduate trainees as a way of growing their own future talent. Before you launch into the annual scramble for graduate trainees, however, you might want to ask, 'Why do we want graduates?' If the answer is 'So that we can secure young, talented and ambitious people' you can then ask, 'How many ways are there to secure young, talented and ambitious people?' In response to that question you might come up with a dozen or more alternatives to recruiting graduates. You now have more options.

- *Reversal* – using the above example again, you might turn the idea on its head by saying 'Let's not recruit any more graduates.' That means you will have to secure your young, talented and ambitious people in other ways, so you have no choice but to generate alternative ideas such as letting graduates 'recruit' you, recruiting non-graduates of similar calibre, developing existing employees, engaging an agency to recruit graduates for you and so on.

- *Features swap* – demand for young, talented, ambitious people is high, so if you are going to compete for them you want to ensure that you

do so with the best possible chance.
Recruitment is not the only competitive
activity. Which other ones can you think
of? Discount retailing, fast-food restaurants,
hotels? Choose a couple of other activities
that involve response to competition and list
how successful companies in those industries
compete. Then see if what they do triggers
any thoughts relating to the issue you are
trying to address. Branding, free gifts and
pyramid selling might trigger novel ways
of recruiting graduates.

Each of these techniques can be used by you working alone or, more productively, with you leading a discussion in your team. Creativity happens better in groups because one person's idea stimulates ideas in other people. The number of ideas grows rapidly.

It is worth bearing in mind an important point that is relevant to the way you encourage creativity amongst your people. There are degrees of creativity. Ideas can preserve current paradigms, stretch them or break them (see the figure on page 89). People can think they are being creative when, in fact, they are simply playing safe by varying a theme. Much depends on the climate you create. People need a safe environment to be really creative.

You can foster a creative atmosphere by:

- getting into the habit with staff of pursuing
  alternatives rather than accepting the first idea

Restatement technique	Example problem	Example restatements
1 Challenge constraints	How to make it easier to drive to work	• How to make it unnecessary to drive to work • How to speed up driving to work • How to minimise the inconvenience of driving to work
2 Generalise the problem	How to improve soft-drink cans	• How to design an efficient drinks package
3 Reduce the problem to its component parts	How to make staff punctual	• How to encourage people to be punctual • How to make it easy for people to be punctual • How to communicate the importance of punctuality • How to reward punctuality • How to discourage un-punctuality
4 Probe for the real problem	How to make senior managers take appraisal seriously	• How to motivate senior managers towards appraisal • How to help senior managers see the relevance of appraisal to good performance • How to get appraisal written into job descriptions
5 Play 'I wish...'	How to raise money for charity	• I wish people were more aware of people in need • I wish wealthy people would make a massive donation • I wish charity administration costs were cheaper • I wish there was less need for charity in the first place

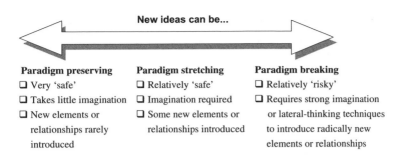

New ideas can be...

Paradigm preserving	Paradigm stretching	Paradigm breaking
❑ Very 'safe'	❑ Relatively 'safe'	❑ Relatively 'risky'
❑ Takes little imagination	❑ Imagination required	❑ Requires strong imagination or lateral-thinking techniques to introduce radically new elements or relationships
❑ New elements or relationships rarely introduced	❑ Some new elements or relationships introduced	

- establishing a rule in meetings and discussions that to earn the right to criticise an idea you must either first state what you like about it or generate double the number of useful ideas yourself
- encouraging people to personalise their work area, dress differently and so on
- cancelling rules and policies that encourage uniformity where it is not essential
- rewarding the generation of ideas even if the majority of them are discarded
- finding someone from another department trained in creative-thinking techniques and asking them to chair some of your meetings
- setting up a creative area, distinguished, say, by music, furniture, colour, lighting and so on, in which people know it is acceptable, even expected, to generate wacky ideas.

Conformity and compliance kill creativity

Work on your own creativity. Here are suggestions to help you.

- Capture spontaneous ideas by writing them down.
- Develop ideas.
- Deliberately relax; make space in your brain for ideas.
- Visualise the problem.
- Play 'I wish...'.
- Find inspiration by breaking routine and habitual thinking patterns; do something different just for the fun of it.
- Play 'Just suppose...'; and be outlandish before you're practical.
- Think beyond conventional boundaries by viewing the problem from different angles and from the perspectives of different people.
- Question everything that is routine or done 'because we've always done it that way'.
- Deliberately probe to get beneath the surface of issues.
- Analyse problems by randomly 'dumping' all your thoughts about them on a large sheet of paper or board.
- Analyse problems by rephrasing them in many different ways.
- Think 'outside the box' by deliberately exposing yourself to information from beyond your comfort zone (specialism,

company, people and so on); build a network of unlike-minded people.

- Find three reasons to support an idea before you dare to criticise it.
- Make your environment more supportive of creativity.
- Develop an insatiable curiosity.
- Use the Walt Disney process. (First, be a dreamer, playfully generating new ideas. Then be a realist, selecting the most appropriate one. Finally, be a critic, looking in detail at ways to improve your idea.)

> *'The future belongs to those who see possibilities before they become obvious.'*

Culture

Culture can be described as 'the way we do things around here'. It is a short-hand way of referring to accepted behaviour. The more accepted behaviour supports your vision, the more likely you are to achieve it – because effectively everyone is working towards it. Initiatives that rely on staff buy-in such as customer care, quality, empowerment, change and so on will have more success if they are supported by accepted behaviour. Such is the importance of accepted behaviour that many an organisational change that looked right on paper or that made sound commercial sense has floundered because senior management failed to address the need to change culture. This has direct relevance to leadership and so is worth examining.

Culture, or 'the way we do things around here', is a product of our:

- attitudes (our feelings towards something)
- values (our in-built priorities)
- beliefs (the concepts we regard as beyond doubt).

Attitudes, values and beliefs (often abbreviated to AVBs) are the product of our experiences. While in some cultures it is accepted behaviour to go all gooey on seeing a cuddly puppy dog, in other cultures it is accepted behaviour to eat the dog. The totally different AVBs are a product of our experiences. In summary, experiences lead to AVBs and AVBs lead to accepted behaviour or culture and culture makes it easy or difficult to achieve your vision.

At work, our experiences are determined, predominantly, by our managers. As a manager, therefore, you create the conditions in which your staff feel it is safe, permitted or desirable to enjoy their work, use their initiative, be creative, perform well and so on. By the quality and consistency of your interactions with staff, you influence their experiences and so develop a culture of teamwork, customer satisfaction and high performance (see the figure opposite).

Here is some food for thought. Past success can sometimes lead to current weakness. You might have been lucky and had the good fortune to be led by a manager with positive attitudes towards staff. In which case, your AVBs will be congruent with high performance. If, on the other hand,

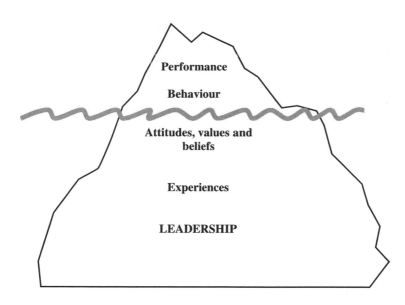

your experiences have been determined by managers with a 'command and control' style of leadership, you may need to address your AVBs. It is worth asking yourself the following questions.

- What AVBs have come from your own experiences?
- In what ways do you need to update your AVBs about management and staff?
- What AVBs are you deliberately developing in your staff? How?

The command and control type of leadership that led to success in the past can leave us with a culture long past its sell-by date. It can make managers reluctant to exchange the security blanket of a command and control style of management for one dependent on consensus and influence. Yet empowerment does not mean giving up control so much as changing the way it is exercised. It changes from controlling people to helping them think for themselves, encouraging them to think positively, to buy into corporate goals, to strive for continuous improvement and to strive for high performance. No leader can insist that people think in this way, but by the way leaders interact with their people and by the examples they set, they can develop productive AVBs, behaviours and culture.

Eventually most managers find that the aspects of staff attitudes and behaviour that are critical to success cannot be obtained by compulsion. This changes the priority of managers' actions from organising workflow and controlling staff to connecting them emotionally to corporate goals. Consequently, you don't spend time with your staff – you invest it in them!

Decision-making

Whether we are working on our own or with a group, we expect our leaders to be able to make good decisions and to help us make good decisions. Make poor decisions and not only is it more difficult to get the job done, your leadership credibility suffers. Make good decisions, however, and not only do you get the job done better, your credibility improves, because people recognise and appreciate the breadth and depth of thinking that led you to the decision. Consequently, decision-making is a crucial leadership skill. Yet it is also one that presents its own difficulties. Here are the traps to avoid.

The problem trap. We sometimes use words very imprecisely and refer to any difficult situation as a 'problem'.
That imprecision can lead us to tackle a problem as if it is
a decision and vice versa. So what is the difference
between the two? A problem is a situation in which:

- something has gone wrong, taken an unexpected
  turn or failed to perform as predicted
- action is required to put the situation right
- you cannot begin effective action until you
  have identified the cause of the problem.

A decision is a situation in which:

- action is required to change or improve results
- you either know or do not need to know the
  cause of the situation before you can take
  effective action
- you have at least two alternatives.

Here is an example. If your motor car breaks down, the
mechanic sees this situation as a problem because he or
she cannot fix the car without identifying why it went
wrong or, in our terms, the cause of the problem. When
the time comes to replace that car with a new one, you do
not have a problem. You do not need to identify the cause
of the situation before you can take effective action. You
simply need to specify your criteria and choose between
the options available to you. You have a decision.

The problem trap, therefore, is where we have a problem
but do not try to discover its cause. Instead we rush into

generating alternatives and choosing between them. We can waste a lot of time, money and effort on actions that can still leave us with the original problem. You can avoid this trap by considering whether you need to know the cause of the situation before you can take effective action. If the answer is yes, you have a problem and need problem-solving techniques. If the answer is no, you have a decision and need decision-making techniques.

The anchor trap. Human brains often give great weight to the first information they receive (initial impressions, estimates, data, comments, stereotypes, past events and experiences), forming an anchor-like reference point for subsequent thoughts and judgements. In some situations, overreliance on this initial information can limit your effectiveness and your capacity to react to change. This trap is especially dangerous in fast-moving situations. You can avoid the trap by:

- viewing the issue from different perspectives, rather than sticking to the one you thought of first
- considering the issue on your own before consulting others
- being open-minded
- seeking information from a variety of people and sources
- avoiding 'anchoring' other people by telling them as little as possible at the start of discussions
- being especially wary of anchors in negotiations.

The status quo trap. People typically have a strong bias towards alternatives that maintain the status quo because it is 'safe', familiar and comfortable. We are especially vulnerable to this trap when faced with too many choices or where 'failure' is very risky or severely punished. You can avoid this trap by:

- keeping goals firmly in focus
- generating alternatives and evaluating their advantages and disadvantages
- seriously considering whether you would choose the status quo if it were not already there
- accurately assessing the costs and benefits of leaving the status quo
- using criteria relevant to future needs rather than to present ones.

The justification trap. Sometimes it can be very difficult making a decision that would prove that a previous decision was wrong. Our tendency is often to make choices now that justify previous decisions. We may do this for our own comfort, to avoid losing face, to avoid criticism and so on. Bearing in mind that most people respect a leader who admits mistakes, you can avoid this trap by:

- openly admitting to previous poor decisions, identifying what you learned from them and sharing that learning with staff so that they can not only avoid the same mistake themselves but also feel comfortable avoiding this decision-making trap themselves
- treating mistakes as learning opportunities

- reassigning problem issues in which you are involved to another person who has no emotional stake in the issue
- listening to the views of people who are not involved
- remembering that no one ever got out of a hole by making it deeper.

The selective evidence trap. Sometimes it is easy to accept or give extra weighting to information that confirms our instinct or point of view. You can avoid this trap by:

- testing intuitive decisions
- using an objective decision-making framework
- deliberately playing 'devil's advocate'
- encouraging staff to disagree with you and creating an environment in which staff feel comfortable voicing alternative views.

The framing trap. Some decision-makers frame a question or description in such a way that it 'channels' the outcome in the direction they want. We are especially vulnerable to this trap when we are making decisions in groups and are afraid of disagreement. You can avoid this trap by:

- restating the issue in several different ways, using techniques especially designed for this purpose (see the table on page 88)
- framing the issue in as neutral and balanced a way as possible
- listening to the views of others.

The estimating trap. Estimating or forecasting in a way that is characterised by overconfidence, overprudence or over-reliance on memory immediately reduces the quality of the ensuing decision but, because of the unquestioning acceptance of the estimates, the decision is not questioned. You can avoid this trap by:

- considering extremes right at the start, then challenging those extremes by imagining situations that would alter the extremes and adjusting your estimates accordingly
- examining and testing your assumptions.

Once you have avoided these traps, you can then tackle your decision.

Decisions need options. If you only have one option you have no choice and, therefore, no decision. Very few situations are this extreme. You may, however, be unhappy with the limited options at your disposal and decide to generate more. The section on creativity (see pages 83–91) will help you. Once you have options, you need an approach to help you avoid the traps referred to above. Here are some suggestions:

1 Describe the outcome you want. The bigger the decision, the more detail you need. Remember to include how you want people to feel. This can be very important if the decision will involve 'winners' and 'losers' (see the section on managing change on pages 74–6).
2 List the criteria, carefully distinguishing between essential criteria and desirable criteria. This is not

as easy as it may sound. Sometimes we regard something as essential only to realise later that it is actually highly desirable. How many house hunters, for example, state they must have a house with a garage and in good decorative order and yet fall in love with a house in need of refurbishment with no garage. If, in later stages of the decision-making process, you find that none of the options passes the essential criteria, you have two choices: you can generate more options or, and this would be my first choice, you can query whether some of the essentials are really highly desirables.

3   Once you have checked options against the essential criteria, some will fall at this stage. Those you have left now need to be checked against the desirable criteria. There are two points to consider here. First, some criteria will be more desirable than others. You can clarify your thinking by numerically weighting them. Second, whereas options either pass or fail essential criteria, they meet desirable criteria to one extent or another. So if you have a dozen desirable criteria of different weightings and a dozen options that meet the desirable criteria to one extent or another, that is 144 pieces of information to hold in your mind simultaneously! It is probably better, therefore, to put the information on paper or on a spreadsheet such as the example in the table opposite.

4   It is essential, however, that you do not allow the scores to make up your mind for you. They are simply a guide. They help you avoid some of the decision-making traps. It is quite possible that you

Desirable criteria				
	Weighting	**Option 1 score**	**Option 2 score**	**Option 3 score**
•	–	–	–	–
•	–	–	–	–
•	–	–	–	–
•	–	–	–	–
•	–	–	–	–
		Option 1 total —	Option 2 total —	Option 3 total —

do not like a high-scoring option, so listen to your feelings. It is quite possible that your intuitive thinking is reminding you of some very important 'emotional' criteria that you failed to take into account earlier. It may be that an unattractive high-scoring option is the rational choice but it is emotionally unattractive. Consider what you would have to do to make it more attractive. This is the final stage of the decision-making process – planning implementation. If your decision involves other people, it is vital that you take them into account at this planning stage. How will they feel about the decision? Will you need to encourage them to buy into it? How will you do that? It is worth remembering that it takes longer to make a decision when you involve other people in the process, but it can make implementing the decision so much easier!

Development

There used to be a time when what you learned at the beginning of your career would see you through to the day you retired. That situation is so far removed from what we now experience that it can be difficult to realise that its residue can still affect us. I see managers giving their own development too low a priority and relegating attention to the development of their staff to a course or two on the annual appraisal form. This means that it is too easy for us to miss out on the links between development and performance, development and motivation, and development and our relationship with staff. Let's look at these links in turn.

Development and performance. Previous sections in this book have emphasised how high performance rests not just on superior technical skills but on superior personal skills. The ability to work well in a team, use initiative, solve problems, make decisions and so on are not always best learned on courses. On-the-job development can be more effective.

Development and motivation. We know from Professor John Adair's work on Action Centred Leadership that performance, teamwork and motivation are all linked. Developing your staff in both technical and personal skills enables them to perform better and to work together better. Success in these two areas has a beneficial knock-on effect on our motivation. We feel better about our colleagues and about striving for high performance.

Development and your relationship with staff. There are several reasons why developing your staff improves their relationship with you. First, most people know these days that job security is not as important as employment security. None of us knows what the future may bring in terms of our job but we know that with the right skills we will always be sought after. Help your staff develop the right skills and you improve your retention of good staff and their assessment of you as a manager. Second, most people value a feeling of progress in their job even when it is not accompanied by promotion. We like the feeling that we can do something now that we could not do before, that we are trusted in a way that we were not trusted before and that we are sought after in a way that we were not sought after before. We are normally grateful to the person with whom we associate those feelings. Third, by using coaching opportunities as a major development method, you spend time with your staff, cementing your relationship with them. In this section, therefore, I am going to give you some thoughts on development that you may not have considered before. (If you have come across them before, you will find it helpful to think about how you can capitalise on them even more.)

Consider how you think about staff development
How do you think about staff development? Do you think of course titles? Do you think of technical skills, assuming that people either have or do not have personal skills? Or do you think about it using the ideas on pages 20–23?

Consider how you prioritise staff development
How do you currently prioritise staff development? Agree with whatever they want? Disagree with every request that does not address a technical skill? Don't know? Here

is a quick and effective way of prioritising staff development needs.

- First, address aspects of performance that could be described as less than acceptable. Failing to address these matters is like trying to make a motor car go faster while the handbrake is still on.
- Second, consider aspects of their work that are acceptable but in which even better performance would have a beneficial effect. Look particularly for those aspects of performance where personal skills are involved, because it is in these areas that it is easy to translate 'working smarter, not harder' into quick results. Look also for aspects of the job that particularly interest staff members or that would add to their self-esteem or transferable skills because this shows you are thinking of their needs in your development of them and not just of how it might benefit you.
- Third, consider developing skills that enable staff to take on tasks from the next level up (for example, work normally associated with the next grade or a more experienced level), that will improve their career prospects or that develop transferable skills. Although this might make them more susceptible to 'poaching' by other managers, you will probably retain their services longer than you would do otherwise, and at a higher performance level. And your reputation as a developer ensures you a good choice of willing replacements.

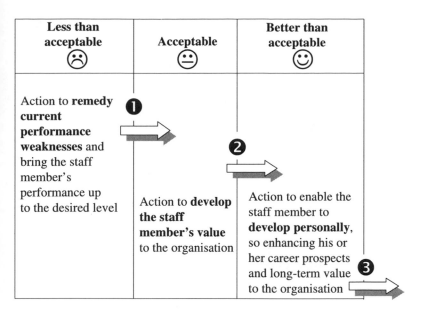

Less than acceptable 🙁	Acceptable 😐	Better than acceptable 😊
Action to **remedy current performance weaknesses** and bring the staff member's performance up to the desired level	Action to **develop the staff member's value** to the organisation	Action to enable the staff member to **develop personally**, so enhancing his or her career prospects and long-term value to the organisation

Consider how you set development goals

I come across many managers who do not agree develop-ment goals with staff. As we all seem to work under so much pressure these days, development is relegated to an 'also ran' in people's attention; it is a nice thing to do but it is not real work. If, however, you agree development goals with your staff, both you and they take development more seriously. Furthermore, if those development goals are rooted in common sense, you can plan in detail how you will achieve them. Which of these development goals would you choose for which members of staff?

1 Observable or measurable increase in quantity or quality.
2 Improved consistency in, or improved mastery of, task.

3   Noticeable improvement in initiative, decisions and so on.
4   Enlarged perspective evident in comments and actions.
5   Evidence of thinking beyond previous boundaries, making sense of ambiguous situations that previously would have caused confusion, thinking both long-term and short-term.
6   Noticeably more creativity than previously evident in response to problems or new situations.
7   Noticeably more and better use of people networks, inside and/or outside the organisation, resulting in better than expected achievement, decisions and so on.
8   Delegation of new tasks; you are able to give staff tasks that previously would have been beyond their ability.
9   They can successfully take on higher-profile, riskier or more important tasks.
10 Anecdotal evidence of personal growth; staff can cite examples of what is being achieved now that previously would have been beyond their ability; of what has been learned, how it has been employed and the results that have been achieved; of being increasingly sought by others for help, advice and guidance.

Consider the development methods you use

Learning is much higher up the corporate agenda than it used to be, but I am not convinced it is higher up the agenda of individual managers. 'Staff development' appears on the list of assessment criteria of too few man-

Chartered Institute of Personnel and Development

Customer Satisfaction Survey

The more feedback we get, the better our books can be! We will send you a
FREE CIPD MOUSE MAT (UK addresses only) as a thank you for completing this card.

Name and address: ....

....

CIPD membership number: ☐ ☐ ☐ ☐ ☐ ☐ ☐ ☐

1   Title of book...

2   Date of purchase: month .... year ....

3   How did you acquire this book?
    ☐ bookshop   ☐ Plymbridge   ☐ CIPD website   ☐ other (specify) ....

4   If ordered from Plymbridge, when did you receive your book?
    ☐ 1 week   ☐ 2 weeks   ☐ more than 2 weeks

5   Please grade the following according to their influence on your purchasing
    decision, with 1 as least influential: (please tick)

	1	2	3	4	5
Title					
Publisher					
Author					
Price					
Subject					
Cover					

6   On a scale of 1 to 5 (with 1 as poor and 5 as excellent) please give your impressions
    of the book in terms of: (please tick)

	1	2	3	4	5
Cover design					
Paper/print quality					
Good value for money					
General level of service					

7   **Did you find the book:**   covers the subject in sufficient depth   ☐ Yes   ☐ No
                                  useful for your work   ☐ Yes   ☐ No

8   Are you using this book to help:
    ☐ in your work   ☐ study   ☐ both   ☐ other (specify) ....

If you are using this book as part of a course, please give:

9   Name of academic institution...

10 Name of course ....

11 Is this book relevant to your syllabus?   ☐ Yes   ☐ No

Call 020 8263 3387 for our latest books catalogue. Don't forget, CIPD members get 10% off!

2299/09/01

Publishing Department

Chartered Institute of Personnel and Development

CIPD House

Camp Road

Wimbledon

London

SW19 4BR

agers. There is little corporate incentive for managers to devote scarce time and energy to staff development despite the rallying cries of senior managers and the lamentations of HR specialists. Hence I am keen to show managers how they can simultaneously develop staff and get the job done.

The workplace development methods shown in the table on pages 20–23 indicate how to find development potential in the work that staff do, and the section on coaching skills (pages 25–30) shows you how to use your interaction with staff as a development tool. Rather than repeat those sections here, I will simply refer you to them. Using these ideas you do not have to find extra time for staff development, nor do you have to cope without them while they are away from work. Learning becomes, as it should be, a natural activity and your bit of the organisation becomes a hive of motivated, high-performing learners.

Consider how you tackle these obstacles to staff development

There are six major obstacles to people's development at work. As you read them, think which obstacles might be affecting the development of both yourself and your staff.

Motivational burn-out due to lack of promotion. Promotion prospects eventually peter out for most people. It can affect the motivation of those who constantly benchmark themselves against others or who believe that progression in a career is an automatic right. It needs a change of attitudes, so counsel the employee and focus on the benefits of their development in their current post.

Motivational burn-out due to lack of challenge. This is the result of overfamiliarity with the job. It need happen to no one. Use the ideas listed above to rekindle challenge, and with it motivation, in the job.

Being 'locked in' by a strength. It is easy to stay within the 'comfort zone' of current success and rely on expertise that meets current needs and gives us satisfaction and kudos. This is also an easy way to be left stranded by events, new technology and new attitudes. So make development part of your management style, emphasise the benefits (and expectation) of continuous learning amongst all your staff. Include those who are content to stay as they are because, as the world changes around them, both you and they will be glad they made the effort.

Being 'locked in' by you! Sometimes we know that developing staff makes them more ambitious and more attractive to other managers. So, either consciously or subconsciously, the fear associated with losing them can make us reluctant to develop them. This requires a change in attitudes. So think about the following points:

- First, your staff are not your personal possession; they are an organisational resource, so you have an obligation to develop them for the organisation.
- Second, as a manager, you have significant influence over a major part of their lives; you owe it to them to develop them.
- Third, you are a major beneficiary of their development. You get their increased motivation

and performance while they are with you, they stay with you longer because they enjoy working with you, and you get the pick of the crop when you have to replace them because good staff want to work with good managers. Your reputation as a manager improves. The quickest way to get promoted yourself is to develop a successor. Not a bad return for a small investment, is it?

Consider the example you set staff with your own development

As Norman Vincent Peale once said, there is nothing worse than people who give good advice and set bad examples. So what development example are you setting for your staff? How many of these ideas are you consciously implementing?

- Develop performance management skills, coaching skills and the skills with which to address poor performers.
- Move away from technical work by delegating more. Gradually increase your span of control.
- Develop interpersonal skills. All the surveys are telling us that successful managers need to be better in this vital area.
- Seek greater involvement in issues critical to the organisation.
- Seek involvement in tasks and projects with greater organisational impact, broader perspective and longer time-scales or tasks that affect the future of the organisation, or a major

part of it, in terms of strategy, culture or new ideas.

- Seek involvement in tasks and projects that require you to bring together resources, people and budgets.
- Seek opportunities to represent the organisation in key interactions inside and outside the organisation.
- Increase the amount of networking you do both inside and outside the organisation.
- Develop your commercial and business skills, because even specialists and managers in the public sector and voluntary sector need such skills.
- Develop key members of your staff for future roles.

Paying attention to practical ways of developing staff is one of those effective and time-efficient activities that enables you to achieve several goals simultaneously. It helps staff have a more rewarding job and a more secure future, it helps the organisation succeed and it reflects well on you and your performance. But only if you approach it correctly. Real development requires more than sending staff on courses; it requires you to make staff development part of your day-to-day leadership style. The ideas in this section will make it easier and more productive than you think.

Enthusiasm

A consistent characteristic amongst leaders is their enthusiasm. Sometimes this characteristic goes higher up the scale to reach determination or even ruthlessness, but we will stick with enthusiasm as being the most useful aspect of the characteristic.

Enthusiasm is contagious. So the more of it you display, the more of it you will see in your staff. When people are enthusiastic, they ignore discomfort, overcome obstacles, work harder, feel better about themselves, have more fun and achieve more. Here are some thoughts on enthusiasm.

First, enthusiasm can wane for a variety of reasons. Listed overleaf are the main ones, with actions to overcome them. Second, apart from extreme situations, there is a quick way to rekindle enthusiasm. *Pretend* to be enthusiastic, particularly to yourself. Just as when you pretend to be happy when feeling down and your mood improves, pretending to be enthusiastic can recharge your batteries. It is worth remembering that we have the ability to choose our feelings rather than to allow situations to determine them for us. Your enthusiasm is within your control.

Setting an example

As a manager you set an example in everything you do. In fact even doing nothing is setting an example. Staff do not have to be aware consciously of your behaviour: they pick it up subconsciously. They see what you do and become aware of what is acceptable behaviour. Their behaviour then follows suit. This process will either work for you or against you. It will either lead to high performance or away from it. It is not neutral; you cannot afford to ignore it. So by deciding what behaviours you want to encourage

Overfamiliarity. When we first encounter an activity it can be fresh, stimulating and challenging. Over time, however, it can become boring, predictable and easy.

Try shifting your focus from those aspects with which you have become overfamiliar to those that have potential to stimulate. Teachers, for example, who teach the same topic year after year could easily become bored with their subject. Instead they shift their focus from the subject in which they are expert to the pupils, who present constantly changing challenges and rewards.

Size of task. The enthusiasm of even the most steadfast of people can falter when faced with a huge challenge. Challenges can be huge owing to their size, complexity or risk. Their size can result in paralysis or inertia either because we do not know where to start or because, despite our efforts, we see no light at the end of the tunnel.

The solution is to break down the task into its component parts. Think of it as a salami sausage, and slice it into manageable parts and schedule the most urgent ones. When working with your team, celebrate the achievement of notable milestones.

Inconsistency with personal values. Over time the nature of work can change. People in the National Health Service, for example, report a shift from patient care to budgetary control. People in education report a shift from the pastoral care of students to an obsession with league tables of exam performance. People in many occupations report a shift from job satisfaction to stress and pressure. The job we started doing may no longer be the job we are doing now.

It may be that you can be patient, recognising that few situations are permanent, and wait for the pendulum to swing back again. Or you may be able to examine the changes and recognise their positive aspects. In extreme situations you may have to accept that the situation has changed to such an extent that your motivations now lie elsewhere.

in your staff, you can determine exactly what example you need to set.

These are the most frequently quoted performance-enhancing behaviours managers tell me they would like to see more of from their staff. You may want to encourage the same performance-enhancing behaviours from your own staff. If so, these are the behaviours staff need to see in you. As you read the list, you might want to identify at least three behaviours you could usefully exhibit more.

- Constantly updates technical skills.
- Exceeds personal objectives.
- Makes a substantial contribution to team objectives.
- 'Runs the extra mile'.
- Can be relied upon to help out with problems.
- Accepts responsibility.
- Solves problems and makes decisions at a level one would expect from a more senior person.
- Owns problems.
- Helps other team members meet deadlines and fulfil customer expectations.
- Sees the bigger picture; understands, and takes account of, implications for others.
- Takes the initiative in communicating to others.
- Manages new, unclear and ambiguous situations.
- Learns quickly from experience and feedback.
- Admits mistakes.
- Applies him/herself well.
- Manages time effectively.

- Acts as an ambassador for the team and company when dealing with customers.
- Has a positive attitude; causes others to think positively.

If none of these behaviours feels relevant to the people you lead, I would recommend you think hard about exactly what behaviours you do want from them. This will not only enable you to set the right example but will enable you to communicate what you want from them as clearly as possible. If you do not know what behaviours you want from them (and please note I said 'behaviours' not 'results'), how can you communicate it? How can you set the example? How can you criticise staff when they do not do it?

> *'Nothing is more confusing than people who give good advice and set bad examples.'*

Feedback

When used correctly, feedback is a very effective motivational tool and behaviour shaper. Understanding how to use it effectively requires an understanding of the pleasure/pain principle.

Both pleasure and pain are behaviour shapers. Our behaviour gravitates towards anything that gives us pleasure and away from anything that gives us pain. Pleasure and pain are relative terms. Other states such as physical comfort and discomfort, psychological comfort and discomfort, and security and fear come into the same categories.

'Pain' therefore can be very useful. It can shape your behaviour so as to save your life or prevent you from physical harm. It does, however, have certain drawbacks:

- Your behaviour can move in any of 360 degrees to get away from it. As a behaviour shaper, therefore, it is a 'wild card'. It has little predictability.
- The farther away from it you get, the less powerful it is as a motivator. In scary situations, for example, the farther away you run from whatever is scaring you, the sooner you can slow down.

'Pleasure', on the other hand, has virtually no drawbacks and plenty of advantages:

- To get the 'pleasure' you have to move towards its source. It is precise and predictable.
- The closer you get to the source the stronger the attraction. For example, every long distance runner knows that no matter how exhausted you are, when you see the finish line you get more energy.

Managers who act as the 'performance police officer' and go around catching staff doing something wrong are trying to use 'pain' to shape the behaviour of their staff. You can see from the description given above how unproductive this can be. You probably know from your own experience that the phrase 'And don't let me catch you doing

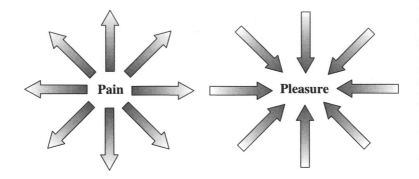

that again!' is unlikely to result in the behaviour the manager wants. If, on the other hand, managers act as the 'performance coach' and use 'pleasure' to shape staff behaviour, they are working congruently with people's brains and are more likely to get the behaviour they want. This does not mean going round delivering a constant stream of gooey praise to staff. The following suggestions will show you how to give both praise and criticism according to the pleasure/pain principle.

Feedback that fails

First, though, let's look at what to avoid when giving feedback:

- *Negative feedback*, because it is contrary to the pleasure/pain principle described above. Even during a disciplinary interview, when 'pleasure' would be inappropriate, you need to avoid negative feedback by being factually correct, specific and descriptive in what you say rather than exaggerating, generalising or passing a personal opinion.

- *Personal criticism,* because it triggers negative feelings, defensiveness and the staff member's fight/flight response. Personal criticism hits the playback button on a lot of negative feelings. Think about this: when parents criticise their children very few of them distinguish between criticism of the behaviour and criticism of the child. With either the words that are used or the inferences contained in the words (or both) the child knows that he or she is wrong. So, 'I asked you twice yesterday to tidy your room yet I see it is still untidy today' comes out as 'What's the matter? Are you incapable of listening or something? You've got to get your act together. Get it sorted. Now!' When you consider the size and power differences between parents and children, you can appreciate the negative feelings generated inside the child. As a result, if you criticise the person rather than the person's behaviour, they experience and resent the negative feelings that you trigger in them.
- *Assumptions* about a member of staff's mental state or processes (unless, of course, you are gifted in telepathy). Telling people that they are lazy or do not care are assumptions based on your observations of their behaviour. You may be correct, but assumptions are 'thin ice' and best avoided when you can stick to the firm ground of descriptions of their behaviour.
- *Generalised feedback,* rather than specific feedback, because the employee is unsure what to do differently or to replicate in the future.

- *Contaminated praise.* Mixing praise and criticism together only confuses the employee. How would you feel if your manager said, 'That was quite good' with the emphasis on 'quite' or 'That was a good report...for you'?

Whether feedback is critical or complimentary, it needs to be specific, descriptive and accurate. It also needs to leave people feeling good about what it is you want them to do. So here are the main steps in effective criticism and praise.

Criticism

Remember that the purpose of critical feedback is to modify behaviour by making people feel better about the performance you want than they feel about the performance you do not want. Its purpose is not to vent your emotions.

- Describe the behaviour/results that you want addressing. Use clear, precise and accurate terminology – after all, they need to be clear about what you do not want. Keep your tone of voice and facial expression neutral.
- Check that you have your facts correct by asking them if what you have described is accurate.
- Listen to their response, including any mitigating circumstances. It could just save you from making a fool of yourself.
- Check they are aware of the desired behaviour/results and, if not, describe them.
- Check that they understand and will do it. See what support they want from you.

Maintain your focus on the behaviour/results you want; don't drift into personal comments.

Thank them in advance for maintaining the standards you have both just agreed.

Praise

Remember, the purpose of praise is to modify behaviour, encouraging more of the good stuff from people by making them feel good about it. It is not to make people feel warm and fuzzy.

Describe the performance or behaviour you have observed. After all, they need to be clear about what you want more of.

Explain how you feel about their performance/behaviour. A simple comment such as 'It makes me feel good to see people implementing so many good ideas', if delivered honestly, has great impact.

If appropriate, you can make them feel even better by asking how they managed to do so well, and where else they can use those skills (or whatever).

Thank them with a genuine smile and eye contact, encouraging more of the same.

There are certain aspects of your behaviour that are crucial to giving feedback, especially critical feedback:

Eye contact. We take people seriously when their eye contact is good without being intimidating.

Tone of voice. We tell a lot from a person's tone of

voice. Hesitation, lack of confidence, impatience, sarcasm, aggression all come through in tone of voice. But so does honesty, directness, confidence, calmness and so on. The other person should be able to infer no negative emotions from your tone of voice.

- *Posture, gestures* and *facial expression*. As with tone of voice, a lot of our communication comes from posture, gestures and facial expression. So they should support the message you are communicating and not allow your feelings and emotions to come out unedited. So keep them neutral.

- *Words.* When delivering praise and criticism, watch out for words that either dilute what you are saying or exaggerate it. Precise and concise communication is much more effective when delivering praise and criticism.

Feedback about you

An important point under the Feedback heading concerns feedback about you. Do you get it? Do you encourage it? How do you react to it, especially when it is not delivered very constructively?

In the same way that customers are in an excellent position to tell us how to improve our service, staff are in an excellent position to tell us how to improve our leadership. Here are some thoughts concerning feedback about you.

- Stay calm and emotionally detached, especially if the feedback is not delivered very carefully.

Sometimes people have to 'psych' themselves up to say something, and they can use words they would not have chosen had they been more rational.

- Explore what they say before responding. This will do more than provide details. It will help them relax and be more factual and descriptive in their feedback and will help you stay emotionally detached.
- Ask them what they would like you to do (if it is critical feedback) or how you could do even more of it (if it is praise).
- Thank them.

If you find that people tend not to give you feedback, a simple yet effective way of getting it is to ask three questions:

- What would you like me to do less because you do not find it helpful to your performance?
- What would you like me to keep doing because you find it helpful to your performance?
- What would you like me to start doing because you think it will help your performance?

Not only do these questions cover all the bases, they are also 'assumptive' questions: they assume that staff do have something to say. Hence they are likely to be more productive than asking staff if they would like to give you some feedback.

You will also find that, having given you feedback, staff have little reason to feel uncomfortable when you give them feedback and perhaps also when giving each other feedback. You can use the same three questions to encourage staff to give constructive feedback to each other, carefully controlled by you to keep it positive and constructive.

> *'The final test of a leader is the feeling you have when you leave their presence; you have a feeling of uplift and confidence.'*

Listening

Listening is important. Very important. Whenever staff are asked about managers they do not like or respect, not listening is high on the list. Whenever staff are asked about managers they do like and respect, listening is equally high on the list.

Listening is not easy. There are two reasons why it can be difficult. First, work pressure can convince us that we are short on time and so we do not have time to listen. This is exacerbated by the huge difference between speaking speed and thinking speed. People speak at an average speed of fewer than 200 words a minute, yet we think at an average speed equivalent to over 2,000 words a minute. Consequently, we 'get ahead' of the person we are listening to and feel we know where their words are going. This causes us to exhibit some of the following signs associated with poor listeners:

- negative facial expressions
- being distracted
- fidgeting

- doodling
- losing eye contact
- closing your eyes
- clock watching
- making 'hurry up' gestures
- interrupting
- changing the subject abruptly.

Second, very few people have been taught to listen. The closest most of us get to being taught to listen is when somebody, such as a parent or a school teacher, says 'Shut up and look at me when I'm talking to you.' At best, this teaches us passive listening. Passive listening means listening with your eyes and ears without taking part in conversation. It is characterised by the following signs:

- helpful eye contact
- looking receptive
- making encouraging sounds and gestures
- making relevant comments.

Passive listening is better than not listening, but it is not as good as it could be when you consider how complex and fragile the communication process is (see the figure overleaf).

First, the speaker has to convert thoughts into words, 'package' them with tone of voice and body language and choose an appropriate medium (formal discussion, casual conversation). He or she then transmits the message. From then on it is up to the listener to complete the communication process.

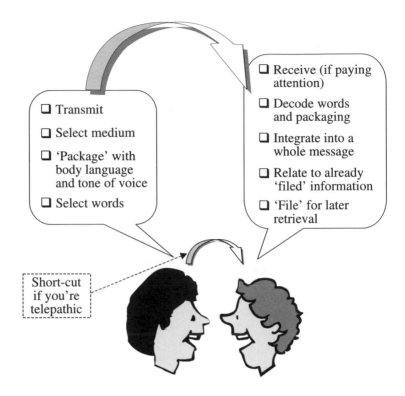

The listener has to receive the message, decode the words and packaging and link them together to form a coherent message. That message then has to be linked to information already in the listener's brain and stored for later retrieval. When you consider how inadequately some speakers choose their words and package their message you can see how much onus is on the listener to complete the communication process. Passive listening leaves too much to chance. Effective communication requires listeners to be actively engaged in the process. They have to clarify words, meanings, feelings, intentions and so on if they are to receive the message accurately. Hence, good-quality, active listening includes all the passive listening signs plus:

- probing to clarify meaning
- checking understanding of key points
- summarising, both to check overall understanding and to demonstrate that the message has been received and understood.

Most of us believe we are better at listening than we actually are. Consider this. A driving school once did a survey asking drivers to rate their own driving skills and to rate the driving skills of other drivers. Apparently, the majority of drivers rate their own skills as above average and the skills of other road users as below average. You do not need a degree in statistics to realise from this survey that we overestimate our own driving skills. If we did a survey about listening skills we would probably get the same results – in other words, our listening skills probably have significant room for improvement.

Are you a good listener? If your staff were asked how well you listen, how would they respond? How many of the 'not listening' signs would they recognise in you? Would they feel that, instead of listening, you appear to be just waiting for your turn to talk?

How do you show people they matter to you; that you are there for them; that you respect, value and appreciate them and so on? The answer is simple – by listening to them actively.

Listening is the highest form of courtesy you can show someone.

Meetings and discussions

People at work have always spent a proportion of their time in group discussions that range from formal meetings to informal corridor conversations. As organisations continue the trend towards being leaner and flatter, delegating responsibility for decisions and input on matters such as quality and using matrix teams, more and more people are finding themselves in group discussions.

You can lead a group discussion formally as the 'chair', or informally as a participant. 'Leading a discussion' does not mean dominating the conversation or telling everyone what you think. It means guiding the process of the discussion, rescuing it when it gets bogged down, keeping everyone on the same wavelength and so on. These are the sorts of skill we appreciate in others, so others will appreciate them in you. Whether you lead a discussion formally or informally, it is an opportunity to boost your credibility as someone who can influence others and thereby establish your leadership credibility.

The 'wavelength' problem

One of the first things to realise about meetings and group discussions is that the potential for misunderstanding seems to increase exponentially as more people join the discussion. The reason for this potential misunderstanding is the range of perspectives there can be on a given issue. Each perspective puts us onto a 'wavelength' different from those of other people in the discussion.

Here are some of the different 'wavelengths' you might have encountered:

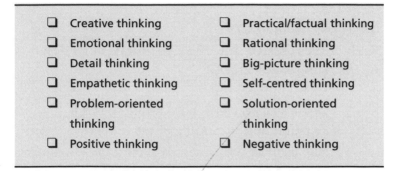

❑ Creative thinking	❑ Practical/factual thinking
❑ Emotional thinking	❑ Rational thinking
❑ Detail thinking	❑ Big-picture thinking
❑ Empathetic thinking	❑ Self-centred thinking
❑ Problem-oriented thinking	❑ Solution-oriented thinking
❑ Positive thinking	❑ Negative thinking

I have listed them in pairs to emphasise the problem. If you are on a 'big-picture' wavelength and people query a point of detail, you can feel they are 'nit-picking'. The other person feels that you are being superficial. If you are on a 'creative' wavelength and other people are on a 'practical/factual' wavelength, they may feel that you are being impractical and you may feel that they are unimaginative. Much potentially beneficial discussion is perverted in this way owing to a simple lack of under-standing.

The way to overcome this wavelength problem is to:

   ▪ 'signpost' your wavelength, especially when you want to change from the previous contributor's wavelength
   ▪ be tolerant and listen actively for clues to the wavelength being adopted by other contributors so that you are more likely to understand their perspective

be prepared to take the lead and co-ordinate the group's wavelength. That way you keep the discussion cohesive.

The right behaviours

Much of the research into effective groups boils down to the following four features:

- *They have a goal.* When everyone shares a common understanding of what the discussion is to achieve they not only have a better chance of achieving it, you can 'refocus' anyone who gets off the track.
- *They agree a process.* If everyone understands how the goal is to be achieved, the discussion becomes co-ordinated, efficient and productive.
- *They ensure mutual understanding.* During group discussions, some people fight their corner very strongly, others are there to represent their section and some have a mandate from their boss. Some just prefer certain wavelengths to others. So it always helps to understand why individuals are adopting a particular line or what their priorities are.
- *They are cohesive.* Some people like to dominate a group discussion, others feel more secure if they say little and others like to start mini-discussions within the main discussion. Cohesive group discussions, on the other hand, are not only more satisfying to be in, they achieve more in less time.

The person who keeps the group focused, understanding one another and following the agreed process to achieve the commonly understood goal usually manages both to influence the decisions and to stand out. They do so because they have established their credibility and because others in the group listen to the points they make. Here are the behaviours that detract from the four features and those that help to bring them about.

	Unhelpful behaviours	Helpful behaviours
Goal and process	No goal or process Conflicting goals Ignoring goal	Suggesting goal or process Referring back to goal or process
Understanding	Excessive talking Being dogmatic Not listening Disagreeing Being negative Changing wavelength without signposting	Probing, seeking information Clarifying Listening Building on others' suggestions Signposting Suggesting alternatives for consideration
Cohesion	Ignoring or losing people's input Dominating the discussion Not participating Starting or joining a break-away discussion	Inviting contributions Co-ordinating thinking modes Summarising input so far Relating input to goal or process Suggesting decisions

Poor meetings and group discussions can be frustrating, unproductive and time-wasting. Good meetings and discussions, on the other hand, are exactly the opposite. We value and respect those people who are skilled enough to make them a worthwhile experience.

Positive thinking

Two leadership characteristics that we value are leaders' ability to persevere in the face of problems and to lift our mood when the going gets tough. Positive thinking (sometimes referred to as Positive Mental Attitude or PMA) is the link between the two.

Positive thinking gives you the ability to:

- see around problems rather than be overwhelmed by them
- think creatively rather than be hemmed in by outdated thinking
- spot opportunities
- see the benefits in an adverse situation
- encourage others to be positive, see the bright side, take action rather than suffer inertia
- be decisive in a crisis.

Here are four suggestions to help you think and behave more positively.

Choose what you focus on

Think about where you focus your thoughts. Do you focus on the negative side or the positive side of events? The most common example has to be the glass that is either half full or half empty, depending on your focus. Here is another example. My son once entered a squash tournament only to find that his first-round game was against the top player in the county for his age group. Understandably he was unhappy at the draw as he was hoping to do sufficiently well in the tournament to qualify for a place in the county squad himself. On the journey to the tournament I asked him how he felt about the draw and, from his answer, it was obvious he was focusing on how badly he would be beaten. I knew that his attitude could affect his performance in the other games in the early stage in the tournament and, hence, his chances of being selected for the squad. So I asked him what his goals were for the match against the county number one. He had none. So I suggested that, as a goal related to winning would be unrealistic, how about, in just one game, giving the other guy the fright of his life.

In squash, the winner is the first to win three games. My son lost the first game by a big margin. In the second game he did better. He came within a gnat's whisker of winning the third and final game, which the county champion had to work hard to take. Even though he was the loser, my son came off the court an inch taller and entered the remaining games of the tournament with great confidence. He learned a valuable lesson. Changing your focus affects your performance.

Is your glass half full or half empty? Do you focus on how difficult something will be or on how much you will learn, on how uncomfortable a conversation will be or on how you want to feel at the end of it, on what people might think of you or how you can help them feel about themselves?

Reframe the situation

An effective aid to changing your focus is the process known as reframing. This means taking an alternative view of a situation to make it easier to deal with. An early-morning car journey, for example, might mean a long tiring day but it also means no wasted time in traffic jams and queues. Another night in an hotel on a business trip might not be as desirable as a night in your own home but it also means you do not have to prepare your own meals or wash up after them.

When confronted with a problem or a major challenge, we can easily be overwhelmed by it. It is at times like these that we instinctively turn to the person who still has a clear head. Reframing can help you remain calm, focused and positive.

Look for the positive

You can deliberately look for the positive aspects even though they may be hard to find. Here is an example. Many years ago I had to attend a meeting and, for reasons I will not go into now, I knew the participants would be after my blood. I really did not want to go but I knew I had no choice. On the car journey to the venue I tried to listen to a positive thinking tape but I could not concentrate on it. All I could think about was how horrible this meeting was going to be. Then a phrase from the tape registered with me. 'There is something good in every situation if only you look for it.' I did not believe it but decided to give it a try. The meeting was even worse than I had anticipated. Many of the personal criticisms were really venomous. There was one guy in the meeting whom I had never rated. However, every time someone said something particularly cutting, he intercepted the words and paraphrased them into more rational terms. Even though there was no benefit to him, he made the meeting much more bearable for me. To this day, when I think of that meeting, my main memory is of this man's good interpersonal skills and generosity to me.

It taught me a valuable lesson: if you look for something you might find it, but if you don't look you definitely won't. It is your choice.

Mental dress rehearsal

Very few situations are totally new to us. We have encountered them, or something like them, before. Consequently, there is often something in a situation that we recognise. That recognition hits the playback button on our emotions and, as negative emotions have greater emotional impact than positive ones, it is often the negative emotions that get 'replayed'. These negative emotions trigger a negative 'visualisation', and what we think about and rehearse in our mind leads to a self-fulfilling prophecy.

Imagine a weight-lifter chalking his hands, pacing back and forth as he stares at the weights he is about to try to lift. Imagine you can hear him say, 'Crumbs, that looks heavy. I'll look a right fool if I drop that.' Would you expect him to lift it? Probably not. His negative thoughts have almost guaranteed failure. Positive thinking alone will not make him succeed, but it will give him a sporting chance.

There is a world-class professional golfer who was leading the American Open tournament by a wide margin when he encountered a problem on one hole. He made mistake after mistake, lost his lead and the tournament. Exactly the same happened the following year. By the third year, everyone was wondering if it was going to happen again. It did. At exactly the same spot. He had probably been replaying this horror over and over again in his mind's eye until it effectively became a dress rehearsal. Sports people in similar situations often seek expert help to learn how to control their thoughts so that their mental dress rehearsals stay positive.

How many times have you 'set yourself up' for failure when, with a slight change, you could have given yourself a sporting chance? When you know a tricky situation is coming, visualise it going exactly the way you want it to go and keep visualising it until both the image and the feelings are consistently positive.

Conclusion – think about the way you think

There is, of course, plenty of overlap between these suggestions. They are just different ways of saying the same thing – we tend not to think about the way we think. All too often, our thinking is left to fend for itself and it is easy to slip into habits of negative thinking. This can be psychologically comfortable because it justifies inertia, giving up and failing. It is, however, a drain on your own energy and the energy of those around you. Positive thinking, on the other hand, leads to action, energy, well-being and the respect of others.

Presentations

People in leadership positions are often called upon to present information to others. This is where your public speaking skills come under the spotlight. Whether you are addressing thousands or only a handful of people, you have a chance to establish your credibility and positively influence everyone in the audience.

Knowing how to give a powerful presentation enables you to excel in a highly respected skill. The following information shows you how to structure a presentation and to give it some 'oomph'.

Mindset of the presenter

Good presenters are positive. They expect to do well and to enjoy doing it. Even if they are not really looking forward to the presentation, they 'pretend' they are. Nerves and anxiety often show in our behaviour. During presentations the behaviours you notice are uncomfortable body language, hesitant speech and apologetic terminology. ('This is just a little slide to show you...' instead of 'This next point is important. As you look at this slide I want you to notice how...'.) The audience wants to enjoy the presentation and are much more likely to do so if the presenter also appears to be enjoying it.

Structure

Good presentations have a discernible structure. There is often a main, recurrent theme. This will be a single compelling message. There will be main points from which spring sub-points. Exceptions and other additional information will be clearly distinguished. One point will lead naturally to the next so that the structure 'flows' in much the same way that a cascading waterfall flows.

Presentation 'tricks of the trade'

Good presenters make use of a few simple but effective techniques:

- Their opening is thought-provoking and attention-grabbing. All audience members have an unasked question: 'Why should I listen to this?' Opening with a thought-provoking statistic, question or observation or reference to the audience's goals answers that question and engages their attention.
- Good presenters speak to each member of the audience. They do so by appearing relaxed, smiling and, particularly, making eye contact with every person there.
- To make it easier for the audience to understand the structure, they provide overview. They deliberately link one section to the next so that, while it is a separate point, it still flows.
- They encourage active and/or passive participation. Participation retains an audience's attention and appears to 'personalise' the presentation for each member of the audience. Active participation means that you encourage the audience to join in by asking them questions (see Presentation style, page 138) or,

if you are demonstrating something, getting them to join in. Passive participation means that you encourage them to join in mentally by asking them rhetorical questions, by using phrases that 'hit the nail on the head' and making suggestions that deliberately trigger thoughts (for example, 'So, think of the last time you were....' Or 'Can you imagine what the effect will be when you...?').

Also, good presenters give their words impact by using such techniques as:

- *Sensory-specific language.* Their words will cause you to imagine what their idea will look like, see what they mean and understand what it feels like. What they say will strike a chord with you, ring a bell or even remind you of the sweet smell of success. Their message will reach the four corners of the world, echo in your mind and receive loud and resounding applause – not the kind of language you would find in a written report, which is probably why it makes such a difference when spoken with conviction.
- *Threes.* We tend to warm to things that come in threes such as 'the Father, the Son and the Holy Ghost' or 'The good, the bad and the ugly'. Speakers find it helps to make their case more acceptable to their audience.
- *Alliteration.* Similarly, a sequence of words beginning with the same sound also seems to register with us. Which all goes to prove that

what you say does not have to be big, bold and beautiful for it to be as attractive as a warm welcome on a winter's night.

Note. A word of caution. When preparing a meal, a cook knows that some spice and herbs will make the difference between an average meal and a great one. They also know that too many herbs or too much spice will turn an average meal into a dreadful one. It is the same with these three tips. Overuse them and your presentation will be pitiful; use them sparingly and your presentation will be powerful.

Presentation style

Good presentation style is usually relaxed and businesslike but, above all, it is genuine and personal. That means:

- They make good eye contact with everyone, including those people seated on the extremes. This is how you let people know you are talking to each of them.
- Frequently, they enter the audience's territory rather than staying stuck behind their lectern or top table. By moving into the audience's territory, you establish more of a bond with them. The alternative is to appear 'stand-offish', distant or in need of security.
- Their style is 'inviting', 'empowering' and informing. The audience thinks, 'I never knew that.' Whether asking questions directly or rhetorically they rarely put the audience on the spot. The audience needs to feel 'safe', that it is

OK to join in, that you are a nice person. They can only do that if you are helpful and positive.

As we tend to speak much more informally than we write, reading from a written document usually sounds formal and 'stiff'. That applies to a prepared speech and also to detailed notes. While all presenters should know their material inside out, they also need prompts, so why not use your visual aids as both a visual aid for your audience and as a prompt for you? This makes it easier to speak 'from the heart' (apparently) without notes.

Their pace is fast. Some presenters slow down when delivering a presentation in the mistaken belief that it will be easier for the audience to understand. That is rarely the case, because when listening to a slow talker the structure is less discernible and our attention wanders. Good presenters, therefore, deliver their material at a fast pace, but because of the clear theme, structure and links, their audience keeps up with them easily.

Problem-solving

As I described in the Decision-making section above (see pages 94–101), we sometimes use words very imprecisely and refer to any difficult situation as a problem. That imprecision can lead us to tackle a problem as if it is a decision. I described the difference between the two as follows.

A problem is a situation in which:

- something has gone wrong, taken an unexpected turn or failed to perform as predicted
- action is required to put the situation right
- you cannot begin effective action until you have identified the cause of the problem.

A decision is a situation in which:

- action is required to change or improve results
- you either already know or you do not need to know the cause of the situation before you can take effective action
- you have at least two alternatives.

If something has deviated from expected results and you need to know the cause of the deviation before you can take remedial action, you have a problem. Tackle it as if it is a decision and you could easily waste time and effort, only to have the problem remain or recur. Problem-solving techniques, therefore, are designed to help you identify the cause.

There are numerous techniques to help you understand situations better. You may already be familiar with Ishikawa (or 'fishbone') diagrams, force field analysis, and mind maps but the technique most appropriate to analysing a situation to identify a problem's root cause is the Kepner-Tregoe technique. Briefly, that technique comprises six steps:

1 Check you have a problem and not a decision.
2 Describe the situation in as much detail as

possible, particularly in relation to its extent and magnitude.

3   Analyse the problem from three angles – *what* is the problem, *where* is the problem and *when* is the problem?

4   Analyse the problem from three more angles – *what* has *not* been affected by the problem, *where* has the problem *not* been evident and *when* has the problem *not* occurred? This puts boundaries on the problem. You may, for example, discover that only two of ten machines have been affected or that everything was fine when the day shift clocked off but, within an hour of the night shift starting, the problem became evident.

5   You now need to examine the difference between the *what, where* and *when* and the *what not, where not* and *when not*, because whatever caused the problem is affecting only some things and not others. You may discover that the two affected machines were serviced between the two shifts or that they have different software or that some of the night shift staff have not attended a certain training course.

6   You now need to do some deduction. Whatever caused the problem has affected the *what, where* and *when* to the *extent or magnitude* described but has not affected the *what not, where not* and *when not*. The answer may, by now, be obvious or you may need more detailed information or, like Sherlock Holmes, you can discount the impossible and be confident that what you are left with, no matter how improbable, is the cause.

You might be wondering whether you need to go to this detail every time you encounter a problem. The answer, of course, is no. It is worth remembering, however, how our natural tendencies make techniques such as this one worth their weight in gold.

Our brains are programmed to recognise situations and to filter out irrelevant information. When presented with a problem, your brain will be searching for an aspect of the situation it 'recognises' and, having found it, will filter out anything that is not congruent with the recognised situation. Sometimes this is fine. Intuitive thinking can be just as correct as detailed rational thinking. If two people win the lottery, for example, does it really matter which one used a rational system to arrive at the numbers and which one chose the numbers on a whim? They are equally rich.

In a leadership position, however, people will bring you problems and they need faith in your ability to solve them. Over-reliance on intuitive thinking or being selective with the information you accept does little to help you make the right action or establish your credibility. Using a rational technique, however, not only avoids these pitfalls, it has additional benefits. Jointly analysing the problem with your staff helps their understanding of the situation, helps gain their commitment to the solution, teaches them how to solve future problems themselves, improves their judgement and so on. Finally, when you consider the pace of change in most organisations, your intuitive thinking can easily produce an out-of-date solution. It is worth investing a few minutes, therefore, in asking the right questions.

> *'If I had one hour in which to save the world,*
> *I would spend 55 minutes analysing the problem*
> *and five minutes finding the solution'*
> – Albert Einstein

Standing your ground

While we like our leaders to listen, we also expect them to be able to stand their ground when the occasion demands. But we like them to do so positively. When aggressive people stand their ground, they just appear stubborn. They dig in their heels and, with their eye contact, posture and gestures, show that they have no intention of listening. When submissive people try to stand their ground they do so half-heartedly, making it plain that they will give way if pressed. You can, however, stand your ground assertively by using the techniques described and illustrated below.

Broken record. This means you repeat the same point, in response to what the other person is saying, as many times as necessary. You can use this technique when you want to remain steadfast on a point, protect yourself from manipulation or encourage the other person to move towards a compromise. You can avoid appearing intransigent when using the broken record by paraphrasing and suggesting a compromise. End the suggestion, however, by restating your broken-record phrase.

Three-part sentence. As the name suggests, this is a sentence in three parts. It helps you show empathy, communicate how you feel and state what you want. You can use the three-part sentence when you want to stand your ground and also encourage the other person really to listen to your point of view. Try to combine the three parts smoothly in one sentence and use 'however' rather than 'but' – it sounds more positive.

Pointing out a consequence. You describe to the other person what will happen if the situation persists. You can use this technique when you need to convince someone you are serious about taking the matter further but would prefer to reach a satisfactory conclusion with them. It is also useful when you need to convince someone to take responsibility for their own actions. This technique requires care because it can be mistaken for a threat. You can avoid sounding threatening by being brief, factual and keeping your tone of voice neutral. At the end of the sentence, return to your main goal and invite them towards a solution.

Here is an example dialogue showing how the techniques can be used.

> *Bill, I'm getting anxious about your part of project x. It was due to be with me the day before yesterday and I haven't seen it yet. Is there a problem?*
> Well...I've been kind of busy lately.
> *I know you have a lot to do. However, your part of the project is overdue and I can't start my part until I get yours. When will it be ready? [Broken record]*
> I'll get round to it as soon as I can.
> *Bill, I can't schedule my work until I know when your part will reach me. When will it be ready? [Broken record]*
> Soon. OK?
> *Bill, I know you're busy; however, I'm very anxious about*

not having the information I need to schedule my work. So I
need to know when it will reach me. [Three-part sentence]
Why is everyone getting at me these days?
It may seem as if I'm getting at you; however, I just need to
know when your part of the project will reach me. [Broken
record]
Just get off my back will you?
Bill, if I can't schedule my work I'll have to explain to the
boss that you won't give me a date. I'd prefer not to have to
do that so please tell me when your part of the project will
reach me. [Pointing out a consequence]
Oh, all right. Let me get my diary.

An important point when standing your ground is to do
so only on serious matters. If you persistently stand your
ground, even on minor issues, you devalue the currency,
as it were. Like the child who cried wolf, people will not
believe you when you most need them to. Assertive leaders stand their ground only when absolutely necessary.
The rest of the time they are flexible. When they do stand
their ground, their strength comes not from a raised voice,
aggressive gestures or adversarial terminology but from
skilled use of these techniques.

Here is a final thought. Often it is sensible to explain why
we have to stand our ground. We have thought the issue
through and have concluded that we have no choice. Our
thoughts have followed the sequence – facts/concerns/
decision. For example, 'Their suggestion means the
proposal will not be ready until Friday, two days later
than we promised the client. That could mean we lose the
business. I've got to stick out for the original agreement.'

When we come to stand our ground, however, our words follow the opposite sequence – decision/concerns/facts. For example, 'Look, John, I can't agree to extend the deadline. I want it by Wednesday as we agreed. Competition for this business is very tough and if we're late with the proposal we could lose it. Sorry.' The chances are that you have lost John's attention after the first sentence because his mind is working on how to counter your decision. If you present the information, concisely and precisely, *in the order in which you processed it in your own brain*, you may not even need to resort to the techniques described above.

Style

Using only one leadership style is a bit like a stopped clock: it will be right twice a day but, the rest of the time, it will be inaccurate to varying degrees. Leaders need to interact with their team in different ways in different situations. This is what we mean by 'leadership style'.

Leadership training is very susceptible to changing fashions and, when a concept has been around for some while, someone else comes along and invents a new way of addressing the same issue. As a believer in keeping it simple, I find the Tannenbaum and Schmidt approach to leadership styles perfectly practical for the points I want to make.

Tannenbaum and Schmidt recognised that in an interaction between a leader and his or her team there is a trade-off between the control exercised by the leader and the control exercised by the team. No one ever has 100 per cent control, because even if a leader gives a direct order, the team members retain control over, for example, how enthusiastically they obey the order.

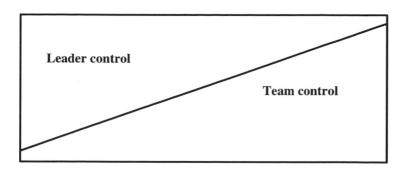

Leader control

Team control

While the model shows a continuum from one extreme to the other, Tannenbaum and Schmidt highlight four distinct leadership styles, from left to right, labelled telling, selling, consulting and coaching. I will describe them below and then make some crucial points about them.

Telling

An autocratic style in which the leader gives specific instructions and monitors staff closely is most useful when the team cannot tackle the task unaided, is unwilling, new or suffered a previous leader who allowed standards to deteriorate. It is the style most people accept in a crisis. For this style to work well you need to:

- be clear and precise about standards, performance targets and expectations
- give detailed instructions
- monitor key performance indicators closely
- use frequent feedback to modify behaviour
- help people over learning problems while being firm about standards.

Selling

A persuasive style, in which the leader gives clear direction and supervises closely but also explains decisions, encourages suggestions and supports progress. It is most useful when motivation is lacking. It is also the best style where a task is non-negotiable but where the team's motivation is vital to achieve the results required. For this style to work you need to:

- develop team skills, monitoring how those skills are implemented
- spend time with each individual addressing standards, skills and motivation
- monitor closely and be directive to keep performance to agreed standards
- listen to the team's feelings but stand your ground in relation to the goal
- reward positive behaviour.

Consulting

This is a collaborative style in which the leader discusses the task and listens to the team's ideas, taking them into account as he or she makes the key decisions. It is most useful when the team has sufficient skills and competence to make a contribution but where the leader feels a need to retain control. That need can result from an imbalance between the team's competence and the risk involved in the task. For this style to work you need to:

- focus on morale and team spirit
- encourage participation, straight comment and feedback

- specify objectives but let the team discuss how to achieve them
- explain fully, and encourage 'buy-in' to major decisions while minimising directives and suggestions from yourself, except in exceptional circumstances.

Coaching

A facilitating style in which the leader allows the team maximum responsibility, this is most useful when the team is competent and has a positive attitude towards the task. You can let them get on with it and use this style as an important part of their development. For this style to work you need to:

- act as a resource that the team can call on when needed
- delegate increased responsibilities
- allow team members to manage themselves once you have agreed clear objectives; allow them to administer day-to-day monitoring and control
- represent the team to others, when necessary tackling anything that interferes with their performance.

These are the four styles. You might like to ask yourself which styles you have encountered most often during your career and the effect they had on your motivation. Consider also with which style an aggressive manager would naturally feel comfortable and with which style a submissive manager would naturally feel comfortable.

Aggressive managers gravitate towards the telling style. After all, they are the ones in charge, their ideas are better than any their team might come up with and it is their job to give orders. The result is that their staff throttle back, display less initiative, delegate upwards and contribute less. This means that the manager has more monitoring and controlling to do. Aggressive managers get the staff they deserve. Submissive managers gravitate towards the consulting style even when it is inappropriate. They will get new, non-negotiable targets from their manager, for example, and discuss them with staff as if they were open to debate. Staff feel conned.

Some managers like to complete questionnaires to find out what their style is. This is a wild goose chase. You cannot afford to be anything other than competent in all four styles. Your strength does not lie in any one style: it lies in knowing when to use each of them and being flexible enough to do so. As a general rule, most managers feel comfortable towards the left of the continuum because this is where they maintain most control. To gain the benefits of leadership leverage (see figure, page xviii), however, you have to move to the right of the continuum. It is at this end that you grow and develop your people, achieve high performance and establish yourself as a credible leader. So why not set yourself a goal to adopt the coaching style of leadership more often than you do now?

Teamwork

See the suggestions on teamwork in Chapter 3, Manager or leader?

Vision

See the suggestions on vision in Chapter 3, Manager or leader?

Suffice it to say here that managers maintain things, leaders change things. To change things you have to be able to see in your mind's eye how you want things to be. Whether your vision is grand or modest, you have to be able to see it in your mind's eye in sufficient detail to visualise what people are saying, doing and feeling. This is the kind of detail you need to go to. If you do not, your mind's-eye vision will be incomplete and, hence, will not help you clarify holistic performance expectations.

Very little on Earth has happened as a result of human intervention that has not existed in someone's mind's eye first. So if you have to, begin with a bit of daydreaming. According to Thomas S. Kuhn's book, *The Structure of Scientific Revolutions*, that is how most breakthrough thinking happens.

5

Final thoughts

If you are a CEO or senior manager

Most people accept that meeting today's huge challenges requires effective leadership at the top of the organisation. They will also accept that high performance is easier when every employee buys into corporate goals. But such is the performance potential of harnessing each employee's ability and willingness to *think* on behalf of the organisation, we cannot leave 'leadership' to a single person or to a few people far removed from the day-to-day influence of employees' motivation.

The challenges are such that we need leadership to percolate throughout our organisations so that every manager has the skills and desire to emotionally connect the people the organisation employs to the results the organisation needs to achieve.

So you might like to consider how high a priority leadership is to you. If, as I hope, it is a high priority, you might like to ask yourself, 'Would managers in my organisation know from what I do that developing their leadership skills is a high priority to me?'

If you are in HR

Increasingly, we hear of HR specialists' desire to occupy a place at strategic levels within organisations, and many HR people are making great strides in that direction on behalf of their profession. I hope that after reading this book you are beginning to realise the performance potential of the manager/staff interface. I would ask you, however, to consider two points.

First, how much more could you do at a strategic level within your organisation to enhance the relationship between managers and their staff? You may, for example, want to review the way promotion decisions are made, the way managers' competencies and performance expectations are agreed, the leadership example set by the senior management team, multisourced feedback on leadership effectiveness, staff morale surveys and so on. That way you can make leadership a strategic issue.

Second, ask yourself how realistic it is to expect managers to learn leadership skills on a single training event. Would it be better to 'unbundle' the leadership skills relevant to your organisation and help managers develop them gradually but effectively?

If you are a manager

I would like you to finish this book with three thoughts in mind. First, recognise the three parts of your job: doing things, managing processes and leading people. Second, recognise the potential for both your performance and your job satisfaction of developing even better leadership skills. Finally, remember the immense power you have to influence for the better the satisfaction that fellow human beings gain from a major aspect of their lives. I would like to think that, after reading this book, you will use that power wisely.

Good luck!

Index